MINIATURE ROSES

MINIATURE ROSES

For Home and Garden

SEAN McCANN

Drawings by Rosemary Wise
With 21 color plates and 33 drawings

ARCO PUBLISHING, INC.
New York

Published by Arco Publishing, Inc.
215 Park Avenue South, New York, NY 10003

Library of Congress Cataloging in Publication Data
McCann, Sean
 Miniature roses.
 1. Miniature roses. I. Title.
SB411.M456   1985   635.9'33372   84–24244
ISBN 0–668–06317–3

Text and line illustrations © Sean McCann 1985

Printed in Great Britain

CONTENTS

ACKNOWLEDGEMENTS

My love of the miniature rose has been fostered by a great many people in different parts of the world and when the time came to write this book they were the people I turned to. Certainly I would have stumbled a lot more without the help of Mr Frank Bowen, a former President of the Royal National Rose Society and the World Federation of Rose Societies. Being Britain's foremost judge and exhibitor of miniatures there is very little that Mr Bowen does not know about them and he gave me the benefit of his knowledge without hesitation. To him I owe a great deal of thanks.

Rose breeders everywhere were extremely helpful, giving me the freedom of their greenhouses to look and ask questions (often awkward ones) about their roses of today and tomorrow. Ralph Moore, the man who really began the minature boom many years ago; Sam McGredy; Pat Dickson; Harmon Saville, Dee Bennett; Jack Christensen; Bill Warriner (of J and P); Jack and Peter Harkness; Frank and Gareth Fryer; Michael O'Dell (of Meillands); Tony Gregory – these and many others never stinted their assistance.

Through the years, many friends who grow miniatures have helped me in so many ways (some driving me hundred of miles to visit hybridisers and nurseries). To attempt a full list is asking for trouble, so I hope those whom I have inadvertently missed out will just put it down to a brain that finds it hard to keep in touch with so many great rose lovers and friends.

So I say thank you to Don and Mary Marshall; Dottie Michelas; Martin J. Martin; Frank and June Benerdella; Jim and Joan Kirk; Vincent Gioia; Fred and Wini Edmunds; Ed Ward; Rose Gilardi; Douglas Rhymes; Howard and Millie Walters; Kasimer T. Niemaszyk; David and June Burton – and so many others. And a word too for my daughter Oonagh who took a lot of the hard work out of this book by doing the bulk of the typing.

To all these true rose lovers and to the memory of a great rose friend, Gerry Hughes, I dedicate this book.

1

HALF THE SIZE

The miniature rose is one of the most adaptable plants you will ever find. You can put it in a rockery, in a border, in a bed, in a pot; plant it in a window-box to brighten a city basement flat, or in a tub on top of a high-rise apartment block; grow it in a garden, a green-house or a small conservatory; you can even use it as a house plant for long periods of the year. It grows as a small bush, anything from 15–60cm (6–4in) high, depending on how it has been propagated, or as a ground-cover plant, a hanging plant, or a climber. It comes in every colour and mixture of colours that you can ask for — laven-ders and greens, whites and yellows, reds and pinks and bicolours as bright as sunshine.

In the past five years, miniature roses have come on so fast that in some parts of the world today more are sold than all other types of roses combined. In Britain, the Royal National Rose Society has seen the entries of minia-tures for its shows increase thirty times in under ten years; in national shows in the USA the miniature entries now outstrip all others. Yet ten years ago miniatures were regarded by many as mere novelty plants. One writer even disparagingly called them 'toy roses'. What a change he would see today.

While the real popularity of minia-tures is of recent development, these little plants were being sold in Euro-pean markets over a century ago — then they were window-ledge plants, sold to be grown in pots and later dis-carded. Where they really began is a secret known only by nature; as Walter de la Mare said:

> Oh, no man knows
> Through what wild centuries
> Roves back the rose.

There is some evidence of miniature roses being sold in Asia and Europe around the 1700s; they probably were developed through various Chinese roses. The origins of the first miniature roses as we know them today are uncertain. The progenitor of practi-cally all the modern miniatures is a rose-red variety called *Rosa rouletii*, named to honour a Colonel Roulet, who spotted its potential when he saw it in a Swiss village at the start of this century. This little rose was then being sold locally as a pot plant, and its com-mercial introduction on a much wider scale set the miniatures moving. But not all that fast; in the early 1930s there were only four well-known miniatures generally available — *R. rouletii, R. indica pumila*, Pompon de Paris and Oakington Ruby. The strange thing

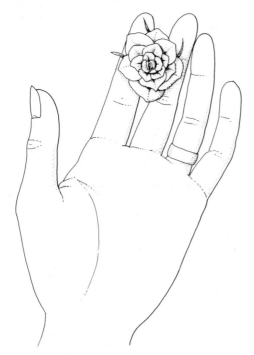

A good indication of the size of most miniatures. At bud size they will be about 12mm (½in) deep, and when fully open, as here, they can be anything up to 5cm (2in) wide.

about all these is that they are very much alike and you really need to sit down and study the plants to find the differences. But, after careful examination, you will probably find — as I did — that Pompon de Paris and *R. indica pumila* are one and the same variety; *R. rouletii* resembles them too, but its blooms tend to be slightly smaller. These three are in similar deep rose to lavender colours, depending on where and how they are grown. Oakington Ruby, which is named for the village where it was bred in Cambridge, England, is red with a slight touch of white in the centre of the bloom.

There were people who saw the opportunities in the miniatures and they set about breeding new varieties using the original four as parents. The real breakthrough came with the arrival in 1935, from a Dutchman, Jan de Vink, of the crimson Peon, appropriately renamed Tom Thumb by

Robert Pyle when he introduced it to the United States. Pyle introduced a number of other varieties, as did Thomas Robinson in England and the Spanish hybridist, Pedro Dot, who had a string of successes that included the perfect little white Pour Toi (also known as For You, Para Ti and Wendy).

Then came the creations of Ralph S. Moore, a rose breeder in Visalia, in central California. He is the father of the modern miniature and his many varieties have swept through the world of roses. He continues to strengthen his string, giving us miniature roses in every conceivable colour, shape and size; varieties such as his yellow Rise 'n' Shine, red-and-white Magic Carrousel and the red Fire Princess are among the top roses today. But the number-one variety all over the world for a long time has been the French-bred Starina. This beautifully shaped vermilion-scarlet came in 1965 from Meillands, the family who produced the great hybrid tea rose Peace, and has consistently been top of the polls since then.

Now the other top rose breeders have decided that they cannot be left out of the action. Famous names such as McGredy (New Zealand), Kordes (Germany), Poulsen (Denmark), Dickson (Ireland) and a great flurry of hybridists in the USA — Saville, Jolly, Dee Bennett, Ernest Williams, Ben Williams — are all offering new roses in the miniature style.

What is miniature style? To many people, a miniature rose is simply a small bush with small blooms — but not to Sam McGredy. This hybridist, famous for so many 'classic' hybrid teas and floribundas over the years, has a special concept of the miniature as a ground-cover plant or, as someone dubbed it, 'a creepy-crawly'. The McGredy idea is that these roses will come as little mounds of blooms to cover awkward spots in the garden landscape — tumbling over walls and down banks, or simply growing under the feet of other roses, thus cutting out the problem of weeding. And alongside McGredy is another hybridist, Onodera of Japan, who was probably the first to win awards worldwide for this type of miniature.

In the busy, changing world of roses there have to be anomalies. There are now a great number of in-between varieties on offer; some have blooms as small as the miniature but grow into bushes that can create mounds 3m (10ft) around. In the magnificent German gardens on the island of Mainau on Lake Constance these are seen to perfection in the Harkness-raised 'Fairy' roses: Fairy Prince, Fairy Changeling and Fairyland. Then there are small plants with blooms that are just too big to be considered miniature, such as Robin Redbreast from Holland's Peter Ilsink. So one problem facing rose breeders today is: 'When is a miniature not a miniature?' The World Federation of Rose Societies will have to determine an answer. But it is not a serious problem because the more roses the world can have, the better.

The real boom, though, is and will continue to be in 'true' miniatures, those mentioned at the beginning of this chapter, the little roses on little bushes that will grow anywhere, bringing their own beauty to places where roses could never be grown before. Children can have them in their own tiny gardens; they can bring great pleasure to the handicapped, who can work with them on a bench or a table. They are easy to manage, and as easy to propagate as geraniums.

Miniature roses came into my life quite recently. I grow about 1,000 hybrid teas, floribundas and climbers in my own garden and up to 1977 there wasn't a miniature there. Five years later, I had an extra 1,000 roses, but this time they were all miniatures. There were times when I was uncertain about them — after all they were only a hobby and they looked like taking over my life. But visitors to my garden always went away with a miniature or two as a gift and I saw the great joy the little plants brought with them. So the miniatures and I struck up a real relationship that had me propagating them, showing them and even creating my own. So much smaller than the garden roses, they seem to have twice the appeal.

2

THE DIFFERENT TYPES

Step one in buying a miniature rose is to find the right plant. Get a good healthy specimen, not one that has been in a shop for weeks and has been allowed to almost die off, for while you can bring a bad plant back to growth it will never be a good plant. A good miniature, given a modicum of care and attention, will be a great addition to your garden.

First of all, notice the difference there is in miniatures. Some plants are very large and others can be tiny. This can of course be attributed to the type of miniature but more often it is because of the way it has been propagated (see Chapter 9 for an explanation of the various methods). The most vigorous are those budded on to wild stock, next to these are the grafted plants and then, much smaller initially, are the plants growing on their own roots. In Britain, you can have your choice of all three, in America I have seldom seen a miniature for sale other than on its own roots.

Own-root plants are usually sold in containers and are growing on; bare-root plants are sold mainly in the dormant season, although these days many growers do pot these on and sell them during the flowering season. The difference will be obvious. The smaller plant will look the most likely to make

a decorative addition to your house or greenhouse while the budded or grafted type looks far more suitable for outdoor planting. But don't be misled. Own-root miniatures can grow on to be quite as vigorous as the budded types after a time, especially if they are not cut hard back. They always remain daintier, though, and are certainly ideal for pots, tubs or containers. The principal method used to grow these own-root plants is to take a finger-length slip and grow it on in a small pot under greenhouse conditions. When growth is well established the plant may be shifted to a larger pot but more often than not it is sold in the pot in which it was raised.

While this growing process is quite labour intensive it involves nothing like the amount of work that goes into budding or grafting roses. These are jobs that generally can be done only in the summer months and require a huge amount of back-breaking work. Budding is a skill that needs great patience and determination. Grafting takes less skill but still needs a great deal of patience and is also very labour intensive. All sorts of mechanical gadgets have been tried out in recent years to make budding and grafting easier but they have failed. So nurserymen have had to look around for other methods that will give the public a better plant; one that can be prewrapped and sold bare rooted is much easier to market and transport. The system most likely to succeed in this area is that developed by the giant Jackson and Perkins company in the United States, whose rooted cuttings are field planted and left to grow on for a year. Then, during the plants' dormancy, they are lifted, placed in plastic sleeves and put into cold storage until they are needed for sale. This way the public is getting the equivalent of the bare-root 'big brother' roses.

But no matter how big this business gets there will still be room for the small nursery where they may sell 10,000 miniatures a year, generally own-root plants. In Europe few growers go along with the American presentation of one plant per pot. The French firm of Meillands has set the style with three cuttings to a small pot. The resultant plants are, of course, bigger and better looking than the single-cutting ones. This also gives the customer the opportunity to split up the plants when they have finished flowering; then they can be planted outdoors or potted on individually. The only problem I have found in this situation is that these plants have been selected under greenhouse conditions and may not do all that well in the open garden; but they should be tried. Certainly they will give years of growth in the greenhouse if cared for correctly and potted on before becoming pot-bound.

In the United States and Canada the own-root miniatures have held such a dominant position that few people would look for a miniature in any other form. In Britain it has been the other way round, with budded plants predominating — growing from cuttings wasn't found to be all that easy in the British climate. Now, however, the arrival of tissue culture will change

Minature roses come in all shapes and sizes. Here is a seedling of my own with almost dahlia-like form, and pure white flowers that open to about 38mm (1½in) in diameter. And it is carried attractively on a bush that is full of light green foliage.

that (see Chapter 9). Much the same can be said for Australia and New Zealand, where several small nurseries are actively producing miniatures on their own roots and no doubt these will soon be the accepted methods of miniature production.

The selection of your miniature, then, will depend a great deal on where you live. If you have a choice between the differently produced types the situation where you want to grow the miniature will be the important point. Certainly I have never experienced any difficulty in bringing on the own-root plants in any garden site.

So much for propagation, but what about the varieties of miniatures that are offered for sale? Here again there is

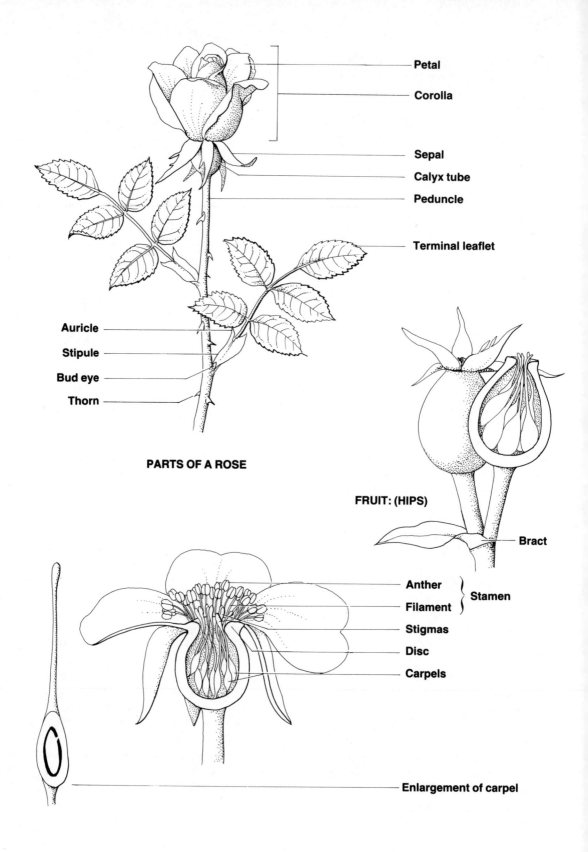

Petal

Corolla

Sepal

Calyx tube

Peduncle

Terminal leaflet

Auricle

Stipule

Bud eye

Thorn

PARTS OF A ROSE

FRUIT: (HIPS)

Bract

Anther

Filament

} Stamen

Stigmas

Disc

Carpels

Enlargement of carpel

such a wide selection that it is better to know exactly where you want to use the plant before you set out to buy it.

There is no doubt that it is the hybrid-tea-shaped varieties that get all the publicity and catch the eye with their perfect blooms. These have everything that the bigger roses have, with the additional benefit of not being as easily spoiled by rain. They also last a great deal longer when taken as cut flowers. The big winners here are so numerous that to name fifty would be to leave out a whole collection that would be loved by someone somewhere. So I will settle for my favourites: Peaches 'n' Cream (creamy-pink), Birthday Party (medium pink), Hot Shot (orange-red), Freegold (deep yellow), Starina (vermilion-scarlet), Center Gold (yellow), Rose Window (orange), and Rise 'n' Shine (yellow).

In the floribunda-type miniatures there are just as many giving sprays of five to ten blooms at any one time. I like the salmon-pink Angela Rippon, although many consider it too big in the bloom. And because of my delight in the mauve colours I have a special affection for a little one called Blue Mist, though this one is not easy to find. But you too will quickly discover your own favourites among the hundreds of varieties that are on offer.

In the bushy plants there are two types of miniature: those that will grow eventually to about 45cm (18in) high and those that will seldom make much more than 20cm (8in). The latter are the micro-minis, the smallest in many cases make a solid mound of blooms only a few centimetres high. My favourite of these is Stacey Sue, a very prolific light pink that does well outdoors, under lights and in a pot — and you can't get a much more versatile plant than that. But there are others too that do well in this category: Littlest Angel (medium yellow), Little Linda (another yellow variety that has done particularly well for me), Sweet Fairy and Pearl Dawn (both light pink), and Si (white). Every year there is another to add to this list. These micro-minis are the ones to use for indoor gardens under lights, or potting. If you keep them well pruned (with judicious pruning, not hard cutting back all the time) you will keep them small. Remember that you don't have to use bonsai methods with any of these miniatures — they are naturally tiny.

Apart from bush miniatures there are also about twenty varieties that can be used effectively as climbers, growing to about 2m (6ft) high and all carrying a good season of bloom. Not all are easily obtainable but as the appreciation of miniatures increases so will the appreciation of climbers. The pearl-pink Nozomi, a five-petalled Japanese miniature climber has been my wonder rose. I have grown it straight up with a support as a climber, allowed it to cascade down from a height, and used it for ground cover and even for flowing down walls and banks where it can easily be hooked into the soil to give a mass of summer flowers. While it has a long flowering span during the summer, its one fault is that the blooms are few and far between after the first blooming. Newer varieties like Snow Carpet, Angelita, Red Bells and Pink Carpet can be used in much the same way. For flat ground cover, they can be either planted in among other roses or allowed to grow in a selected spot in your patio where the long stems will spread out and provide a splash of colour. And don't forget the hanging basket. Miniatures of the climbing and ground-cover variety do well here too, but make sure that you get as deep a basket as possible to take the root length. The baskets need not be restricted to the climbers and ground coverers; there are other varieties that do well such as Sweet Fairy, Green Ice (white with touches of green, especially under lights) and Red Cascade (dark red).

If you want something that is really different, try some of the miniature moss roses. The leader in the production of these is the inimitable Ralph Moore of California. He began it all with a rose called Fairy Moss that he introduced in 1969. This is a medium-pink bloom with a really mossy bud (covered with lots of tiny resin-coated bristles), a trait brought in by the introduction of the old garden rose William Lobb with the miniature strain provided by the orange-red New Penny. From these two varieties Ralph Moore went a long way to producing the superb, light-pink Dresden Doll, and others with mossing around the bud. This was taken up by other breeders, and varieties from Jack Christensen at

Appropriately named, Single's Better is a 5-7 petalled rose from Harmon Saville that is both mossy and fragrant. It's thorny, bushy and makes a good basket subject – a new rose with an old look.

Armstrongs also entered the field, with a great depth of colour. Now you can have moss roses in red, pink, white and yellow, and there are a lot more still to come — mixtures of all colours are among the seedlings produced by Ralph Moore. The most exciting I saw was striped purple, mauve and silver, and one can only hope that it lives up to the promise it showed as a seedling.

Many miniatures hark back to this image of old garden roses, as do the five-petalled varieties that remind many people of the wild rose. These single roses please me as much as the ones with the lovely high-spiralled pencil-sharp centres. A mass of bloom on the vigorous and easy to grow Simplex is something to see; the buds begin with a touch of apricot and open to white blooms with a bright yellow centre. Popcorn, with clouds of white florets, and Single Bliss, a mound of red-and-white-eyed blooms, are both also very hard to resist.

Miniatures grown as standard or tree roses can be very effective too, in a large pot or planter, in the centre of a bed or backing up a border of miniatures. The stems or trunks are usually about 45cm (18in) tall and need to be staked. If you want a specimen plant for a patio or balcony look for one of these. You won't find every variety budded on to a tree; nurserymen select the varieties that will give the best mound-type head of flowers — look out for Green Ice, Golden Angel, Fire Princess and Darling Flame for really beautiful colour. But, again, don't let my suggestions limit your choice; if you like a variety go for it in either bush or tree form.

Often sold alongside the miniatures are polyantha roses — pretty but far less interesting. These are generally pot grown and usually brought along in heated greenhouses. Brought into the home they last a very short time and do little to help the reputation of the sturdier and much better miniatures. The difference is not easy to describe but generally the polyanthas are red or pink or, occasionally, white. The flower form is floppier and less shapely than that of a miniature. The miniature is a much daintier plant, with bloom and foliage proportionately small. The flower form of the miniature too is generally much closer to the form we have come to expect in hybrid teas and floribundas. There are very few polyantha roses however and those that have been introduced in recent years will not interest us here.

You may see 'patio' or 'miniflora' roses offered for sale; don't let these confuse you. Basically they have blooms that are in the style of the miniature but generally open a good deal larger. Where do the patio/miniflora roses fit? In fact, they fit exactly into the same situations as miniatures and can be grown in the garden or in containers. But remember they generally grow much bigger than miniatures.

The world of the miniature rose contains as many different types as the world of the bigger roses, so know what you want before shopping.

Below is a brief selection covering the different categories.

Hybrid tea style
Perfection in a single flower: Starina (vermilion-scarlet), Rise 'n' Shine (yellow), Magic Carrousel (white, red tipped), Beauty Secret (cardinal red), Jean Kenneally (apricot), Gloriglo (orange-yellow), Party Girl (apricot blend), Judy Fischer (pink), Darling Flame (bright orange), Peaches 'n' Cream (pink blend).

Floribunda style
While most miniatures will produce three and more blooms to a stem these have the look of the free, flatter bloom of the floribunda: Cinderella (white), Blue Mist (lavender), Popcorn (white), Stacey Sue (light pink), Little Buckaroo (red), Anytime (orange), Orange Sunblaze (orange).

Old garden rose style
With the quartered or the single look: Mimi (medium pink), Pompon de Paris (rose red), Memory Lane (light pink), Simplex (white), Single Bliss (red, white eye), My Sunshine (yellow).

Moss rose style
Lots of tiny prickles right up around the bud of the flower: Dresden Doll (light pink), Fairy Moss (medium pink), Lemon Delight (medium yellow), Honest Abe (dark red), Heidi (medium pink), Honey Moss (white).

The eye-catchers
Roses of a different colour. There will be many more to come but watch out for: Earthquake (red and yellow stripes), Stars 'n' Stripes (red and white stripes), Fools Gold (gold, reddish reverse), Mood Music (orange blend), Angel Darling (mauve), Lavender Lace (lavender), Blue Mist (lavender), Green Diamond and Green Ice (both white with hints of green).

The ground huggers
Another range that is likely to expand rapidly in the next year or so. This style really began with the Japanese-raised Nozomi, and using this as a parent hybridisers have produced many new varieties. These can also be used as climbers or for hanging baskets. The first of the Sam McGredy roses in this style are Angelita and Snow Carpet. For very low-growing but less lax plants go for Bambino (pink), Woman's Own (pink), Swinger (deep yellow), Coral Treasure (rich coral).

3

WHERE TO PLANT THEM

If, like me, you have a rose garden you will, of course, find many opportunities to use miniatures. During the past few years I have used them on a patio in great numbers. I bring them on at the bottom of the garden and they always provide substitutes for those that have just finished flowering, thus giving constant colour near the house. In my greenhouse there are always a few plants with blooms, in the darkest days of winter as well as summertime, and they are grown there without any heat whatsoever. Outside there is a special bed where I grow some of my own varieties; these are plants grown on from seed harvested in my own garden, something that anyone can do (see Chapter 10). Many other miniatures are used as foot companions to bigger roses (do plant them on the sunny side where they are not shaded by larger plants) and in one bed a large number of the pink miniature Angela Rippon surrounds the deep red floribunda Korona; between them the bed is only out of colour between January and May, the normal resting period for roses in this part of Europe. I also use them in a shrub border where Mr Bluebird and Baby Masquerade give spot colour through most of the summer and autumn.

There are other places too where I have used miniatures with great success: in raised beds, for instance, and pegged down along banks and slopes they are really eye-catching. Climbing miniatures are also successful in many places — even climbing up to the gutters! Being light, they will not pull pipes down as many other climbers would.

My experience shows that miniature roses are often more versatile in a small garden than full-sized varieties. In the smaller space where you want to provide some sort of landscaping you will find that their compact growth fits ideally into smaller planning ideas. If, for instance, you have a pond in your

You love it or hate it! I'm an admirer of this miniature climber Nozomi (it's Japanese for Hope). Put it along the ground, in a pot or a basket, and it will give clouds of small shell-pink blooms for a long time during the summer. It is also the parent of many of the newer ground-cover roses that are available today. Introduced by Gregory's of England from its Japanese raiser Onadera, it has been one of the best selling varieties of its type for years. (*Gregory Roses*)

One of the world's top miniatures, Darling Flame. It has been a very influential variety for many years at British shows, despite being bred in France (where it is called Minuetto). It is also a very good garden variety, and is shown here growing in Baden Baden, Germany. (*McCann*)

223
ZB
Minuetto
Meilland
1971

garden why not grow your roses down a man-made bank, brushing the water? Or even where you have only a wall to look out on why not grow a number of miniatures in pots and hook them on the wall — providing that it gets a fair amount of sunshine. If it gets limited sunshine, paint the wall white so that there is more reflected light and you will find that they make a lovely sight. The smaller varieties of minis will blend well with plants such as dainty violas. Once you start growing miniatures you will find that they have endless applications in the garden: edge, dwarf hedge, border and bed sum up some of the places where they can be used, not forgetting the whole range of patio situations.

Take edging first. When you have a border of full-sized roses you will find that after a few years they can become a bit leggy, no matter how well they have been pruned and cared for. Provided the soil is in good condition (see page 39) the answer is to plant miniatures along the front of the border at the feet of the bigger roses. They quickly conceal the leggy, woody pieces and provide their own splash of colour along the way. For this you need to use the lower growing types; some varieties such as Magic Carrousel, for instance, tend to grow too tall for this situation. Select the shorter, bushier types or make sure that any others you use do not get out of hand. You can do this by pruning well in the spring and then when taking blooms in the summer, cutting almost at a pruning level again.

As edging plants miniatures are certainly effective, especially the ground-

Honest Abe is the name of this American variety that should be included in anyone's list of the moss miniatures. It's healthy, bright and a good grower. Produced by Jack Christensen of Armstrong's. (*Armstrongs*)

cover plants like Nozomi, Temple Bells, Snow Carpet and Angelita. Soon after the arrival of Snow Carpet, a very pretty little white rose, I made the public statement that it would be a wonderful plant if it only flowered! Since then, rose growers everywhere have taken great pleasure in showing me their Snow Carpets, a mass of white blooms in most cases. All I can think of is that in that early batch of bushes I got a dud. Angelita is a shade on from Snow Carpet in a very light yellow and Sam McGredy, who bred both of these roses, promises much deeper colours in the near future. Placed along a pathway these ground-hugging types are value for money. I have about ten plants of Nozomi along my driveway and they have grown into mounds of beautiful summer flowers. They have the added attraction of not catching on clothes when people walk too close to them. If other colours are what you need try the light pink Stacey Sue, the deeper pink Perla de Montserrat or the oddly coloured Green Ice.

The bright red Fire Princess is one of those really versatile miniatures. It grows into a lovely bushy plant and makes an ideal small hedge. A hedge of miniatures can be very effective and is ideal for dividing a garden, because being low growing it will not rob the rest of the garden of sunshine or light and gives a lively strip of colour. The bright gold, red and pink blend of Baby Masquerade, for instance, is something to see. To get a massed effect the plants should be placed about 22cm (9in) apart or, better still, in two rows, staggered, with 22cm (9in) between plants, and 20cm (8in) between rows. Of course, in a situation like this they do need extra feeding but they seem to get along with one another quite happily. Disease is seldom a problem with closely planted varieties

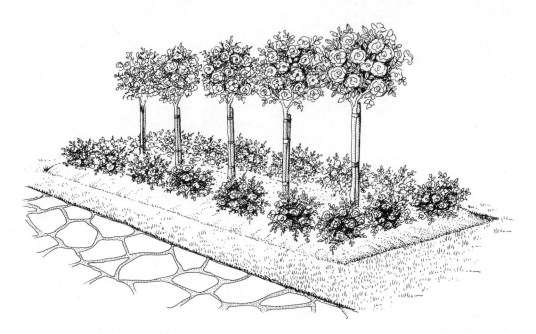

Bedding that's a pleasure to behold, with edging of small bushes and centrepiece of standard (or tree) miniatures up to 60cm (2ft) high.

because when you spray all the fungicide goes on the plants and not on the ground.

Beds of miniatures can be very attractive, especially if you use a standard or tree rose in the centre. Again, the plants should be about 22cm (9in) apart in staggered circles within the bed to provide a low mass of colour all summer long and plenty of blooms to pick for arranging. My only rule on this is to keep beds to one colour and one variety. If you try to mix them you will get a hodgepodge of different sizes and plant shapes that will spoil the whole effect. If you want to grow different varieties together then the place is in a border or rectangular bed; just remember to make sure the low ones are in the front and graduate them in size towards the back. If you need more height at the back, the tree roses will be very effective.

In a rockery you will need to select the varieties with special care. The best effect I have seen was where little groups of three of the same variety were used throughout a rockery which was devoted to plants of all types. An ideal miniature for this site is Benson and Hedges Special (an impossible name for a rose, but probably a highly commercial one), a low-growing yellow that stays quite small. It is one of the newer varieties that have been distributed effectively throughout Britain grown by tissue culture. This propagation method will be used more and more by growers of miniatures because of the speed of production — one new plant can produce something in the region of 10,000 identical specimens in eighteen months, whereas propagation by budding, grafting or cuttings takes years to establish a new variety on the market. Born Free, orange-red, and Red Beauty are two others that come high on my list of ideal rockery plants. Single Bliss has a single bloom, red with a white eye, that sits like a little pompon of flower and is one of the best of the newer varieties for this situation.

For the novel, eye-catching plant there will be plenty of competition in

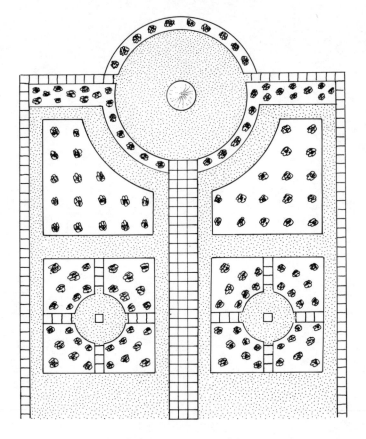

the next few years. The striped generation is well and truly upon us and is likely to catch all the attention. This began with Stars 'n' Stripes from Ralph Moore, a bright red-and-white-striped flower. Although the colour is attractive the variety doesn't produce enough blooms for me. Later plants such as Strange Music rectified this and then Earthquake came along, with its masses of yellow and red blooms, no two flowers of the same colour. And you will hardly ever see as lovely a plant when it is in full bloom as Popcorn, white with a yellow eye. Many more will follow. These varieties grouped in threes anywhere in the garden will make a striking display.

When grown in raised beds with the flowers at eye level, miniatures are a spectacular addition to any garden. The top of the bank is the natural position in this case. Terraced walls (about

A very formal plan for a garden of miniatures. The most effective method is one variety to a bed, but the two square beds in this plan could take as many as eight varieties – one to a section. To give height, miniature standards or bushes planted in urns would be effective. Gravel could be used between the beds to eliminate the chore of grass cutting, but if grass is preferred, make sure there is enough room for the lawn mower between the beds and the walks.

60cm (2ft) high) used as dividers or for flanking a row of steps in the garden can provide a good bedding situation, with the top providing an opportunity for the trailing varieties such as Red Cascade, Snowball (Angelita) or Snow Carpet to fall down naturally and the base taking the taller varieties such as Judy Fischer (deep pink), Easter Morning (white) or Fire Princess. Provided such raised beds are not too wide they are easy to work with and keep clean.

21

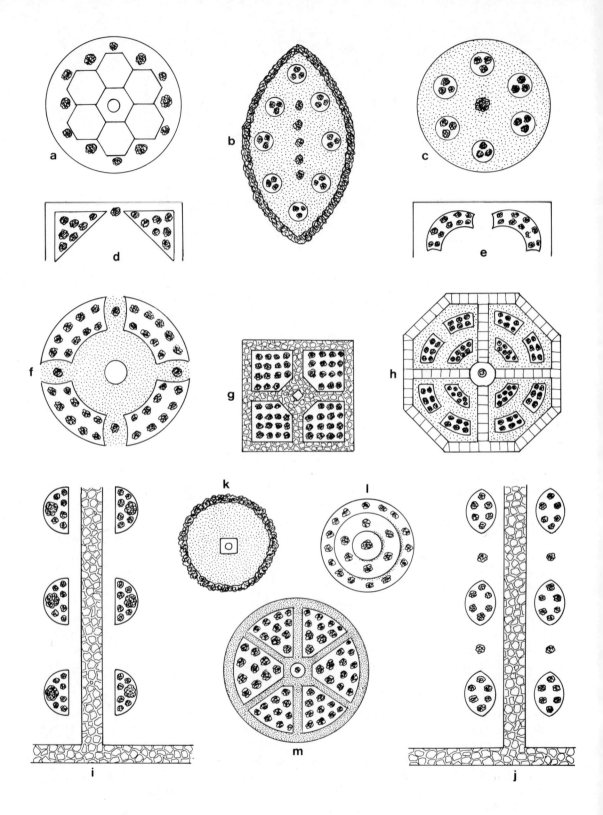

A patio featuring a raised bed of miniatures and some miniature rose trees. Give the trees a good-sized pot or planter to allow the roots to settle and grow and also to keep the plant safe during high winds.

(*Opposite*)
Beds, beds and more beds, plus some special plantings for corner sites in small gardens. (a) Centrepiece – I have a large urn in the centre, with a mixture of miniatures growing around the patio slabs. (b) Within a small planting area there are eight small beds of three bushes each and then some miniature standards in the centre. Gravel can be used instead of grass, and a miniature box hedge can be planted around the area. (c) A circular planting similar to (b). (d and e) Corner plantings for a very small area – also suitable for the edge of a patio. (f, g and h) Complete miniature gardens, taking up the minimum of space and providing the maximum opportunity to try different varieties. To get the widest range of varieties it is better to use a number of small beds as in (h). (i and j) Miniatures make perfect subjects for placing beside pathways or driveways. Each bed could have a standard miniature as in (i) or these could be planted between the beds as in (j). (k) A ring of roses planted closely together give a mass of blooms (one variety). (1) Three-way circle. The central circles could be raised in steps. (m) Six beds to show off six of the best varieties all together.

If your mind turns in the direction of keeping your little roses as specimen subjects in containers, then the opportunities are endless. The size of the pot depends entirely on the size of the plant. I have some miniatures growing in 5cm (2in) pots, others in 30cm (12in) or even bigger containers. Long roots will obviously need deeper space to grow. So look for short-rooted plants, and this is where the own-rooted varieties come out on top. They also have the advantage of never suckering; any growth coming from the bottom will be true to the rose. A miniature in a pot will develop a great mass of fine roots, as opposed to the garden variety which will often have a long straight root with very little fibrous growth. So you will have to watch the plant does not get too big for the pot. If it does you can always trim back the roots, but I like a lusty good-growing miniature as well as the true, tiny plants, so I just pot on to a larger container.

A gallon bucket can make a home for a miniature. It can be less expensive

An ideal way to plant out on a sloping site. For the best effect use one variety on each level – and do make sure that you know the final heights of each variety and put the tallest growers at the top.

An eye catching planting of Nozomi clambering over large rocks (at the Liverpool International Gardens).

to purchase than the equivalent-sized pot and all you have to do is to make some suitable holes in the bottom. It is also a good idea to make holes along the side of the bucket about 2.5cm (1in) from the base in case it gets waterlogged or obstructions at the base stop the water draining away. Take a red hot poker and burn the holes in the plastic. But don't do this in the house and don't do it near children — don't even let them see you doing it! (Warnings about taking safety precautions when children are around cannot be

repeated too often. I am all too aware of things that have happened in my own garden. The most horrifying occurred when I was pruning some miniatures and one of the children crawled up and took hold of the stem just as I snipped. Fortunately the resulting cuts were only superficial — but what a disaster it could have been.)

If expense doesn't matter then there is a wonderful collection of containers on the market and anyone's patio or yard can be a showplace. But good effects can be obtained at little or no cost. For instance, a good china teapot with a cracked bottom now makes a charming plant pot; I have miniatures in an old boot; in litre wine bottles cut in half with the edges well smoothed; in buckets galore; and in a piece of old tree stump gouged out and filled with plant mixture. And I have boxes that could well double as window-boxes, though modern houses seldom seem to have window-ledges. Large tubs (such as cut-down old wine casks) will take

five or six plants. They will withstand much heavier frosts than normal pots and they won't need replanting for years. Probably the most effective use of miniatures I have seen was in one of those lovely old streets in Pimlico, London, where the basement windows were decked with window-boxes filled with plants. You looked down from the railings into a box of beautiful blooms.

Growing in containers does need a special technique. The roots will need room to work and space to grow, so a good depth of soil is necessary. Make sure that there is adequate drainage in the container; pieces of old broken crockery or old clay flower-pots will be admirable. Feeding and moisture are vital to success.

The soil that you use will depend a

25

A simple patio planted with different varieties
of miniatures. One variety in each space is best,
otherwise the different growth of each variety
can make the small beds look very untidy.

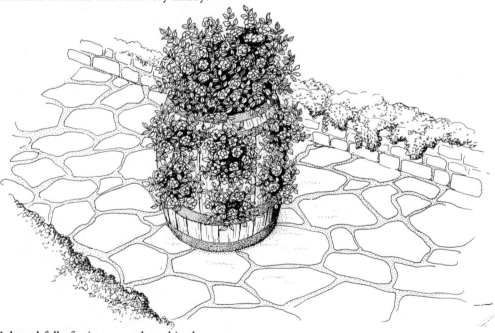

A barrel full of minatures, planted in the same
way as a strawberry jar (which can also be effective). The barrel must be well drained and kept
well watered so that the plants at the bottom
receive enough moisture.

great deal on local conditions, but there is a wide range of potting mixtures available. Get the best you can and most of them will give adequate nourishment for the early part of the rose's settling-in period. After that you must add some sort of food. The newer, long-lasting fertilisers, that come in a sort of granular form, added to the pots at a low rate, will give all year round feeding and I usually add them to the mixture in the second year of growth. Make a few holes around the rose and drop a few pellets in — it's as simple as that.

But each year, too, you will need to look at the pots and possibly even knock the plants out and look at the roots. There are some decorative pots that don't allow for this because of their shape. In this case, the rose's appearance is the only gauge; if it does not look healthy knock it out in case some pest has decided to form a colony there. Have a look at the Trouble-shooter's Guide (see Chapter 8) for individuals that cause havoc (my own little plague was caused by the vine weevil). But if the plant looks to be growing well and quickly enough, then just rake away the top few centimetres of soil and add new well-enriched potting compost. If the roots are coming out of the bottom then it is time to give a little more compost at the base of the pot rather than at the top. A good healthy plant will have clean white rootlets, alive and thriving; an unhappy plant will give its warning with limp, brown, hairlike roots. Lack-lustre roots need a tonic, just as lack-lustre hair does. The tonic can be a good soaking and then when the plant has absorbed a fair amount of the water you can add a small amount of fertiliser either mixed in water or as a powder.

All this is merely a case of looking at your plants and enjoying them. If you

This is just an ordinary basket painted to look like stone, but it makes an ideal growing spot for miniatures.

Hanging baskets can be very effective with miniatures. Pick the varieties that are specially suggested by growers for this situation – low growers with thin growth are best.

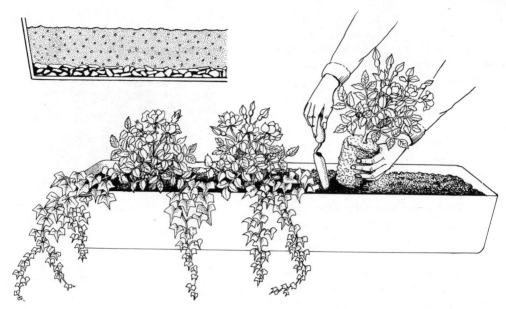

Window boxes need special consideration. Line the bottom with broken crocks or large pebbles to help drainage and then fill with a good compost. Small trailing plants can be used if trailing miniatures are not available.

really take an interest in them you will see the problems coming on and you can do something about them before it is too late. It is when problems are allowed to go on that plants become a headache.

Don't forget that roses you grow in pots are mobile. You can move them anywhere around the house, the patio or the garden; you can bring them indoors for a short while (miniatures as house plants are discussed in Chapter 4); and if you move house you can take them with you.

There is also another area where miniatures can be grown. Still in their pots they can be dropped into a part of the garden that may need additional or spot colour for a short while. Just dig out a hole, drop the pot in and cover it with a few centimetres of soil. You can then take it out whenever you have to make a change. Part of my garden is very vulnerable to flooding, and here I plant miniatures in pots from spring

onwards and take them out in late autumn or early winter, when the flooding possibility arises. That way they can grow on without stopping and are kept out of a muddy situation which they don't like.

Miniature roses have certainly provided opportunities for gardeners on the widest possible scale or for those who want to grow them merely as small decoratives. They are also the perfect plants to grow when age creeps up and limits outdoor gardening. Then the little plants can be handled individually in small pots to give great satisfaction with little physical effort.

Children, too, love miniatures — but a word of warning. Don't let them try to plan tiny gardens with them; it won't work. Few roses will stay for very long in pots that are smaller than 8cm (3in). However, planted in a special corner of the garden they do provide children with a very good introduction to nature. Many varieties can be found that have few if any thorns or prickles: a look at the plant will quickly reveal that while most miniatures have soft prickles behind the leaf, many have none of the traditional rose thorns. The very small plants, such as

28

Cinderella and Si, will always be appreciated. Bambino is very dainty too, though it does have prickles — not enough to damage a child but enough to bring tears if care is not taken. Two of my other favourites, Little Linda and Littlest Angel, also make a good starting point for children. The plants are robust and will stand a lot of childish abuse that would not be tolerated by a more tender, softer-growing or tuberous plant. And where is the child who doesn't like to give a present? The cuttings of these miniatures root so easily that there is little bother in growing them on into very acceptable small plants.

For many of the reasons given above, elderly or handicapped people will love miniatures too. If confined to the house, or even to a wheelchair, they can still actively become involved in growing and propagating them. A fairly low desk or table is all that is needed to take a number of potted plants. I know one man who has three wooden trolleys that are always laden with miniature rose plants. The plants can be grown on, as in the garden, by the provision of a bench that can hold soil to a depth of 15–22cm (6–9in).

The whole saga of the rose can thus be worked by one person with just a few plants. These can be inter-bred to give hybrids that no one else will have (and maybe produce a world beater); they can be grown from cuttings; they can produce blooms to make small bouquets — all this without moving further away than to a sunny window that can carry a window-box or some pots.

Someone restricted to a wheelchair will find it easiest to work at a desk

A bed of miniatures around a sundial makes an effective centrepiece for a garden or patio. In a situation like this, try to select varieties that will grow to the same height, and most striking of all, plant varieties of the same colour.

with a wide enough central area for the wheelchair to move in close to the work-top. Three drawers down the side can hold everything that is needed: soil in plastic bags, labels, pencils, scissors, fertiliser and foldaway black plastic pots. The desk top will hold a good number of plants which can be grown in lightweight pots or trays and are easily movable. It is the sort of hobby that can bring one back time and time again.

Checklist for bedding schemes
Keep the following points in mind when planning your miniature rose garden:

●A sunny, well-drained site is the first essential.

●Raised beds give you a better chance to see the blooms at their best.

●Beds can be laid out in any shape or pattern you require, but have them near a watering source, especially if you live in an area where the midday sun really burns.

●For centrepieces in any bed consider the small standard or tree roses to give height and draw the eye.

●Don't mix varieties in beds. This is vital where miniatures are concerned because they do vary so much in height and vigour.

●To make a large bed look really effective, plant a number of smaller beds within the large one. Small circles, big enough to take three to five miniature plants of one variety, look attractive.

●Finally, consider your paths among the little roses. Very wide paths look badly out of scale and so does rough grass. The best scheme I have seen was where each small bed was surrounded with fine gravel that provided a dry walkway and only needed weeding occasionally. A paved area also looks good. Remember that with narrow grass paths the problem will be how to keep the grass cut.

4

GROWING THEM INDOORS

Do miniatures thrive as house plants? That is a leading question posed frequently by people who have heard differing stories about the roses' ability to bloom indoors. Like so many other gardening questions it has to be answered with 'it all depends' — ie on which varieties you use, on how they have been propagated, and on the conditions you intend to provide.

First of all let us look at the normal indoor situation. There are many miniatures that will do well inside for upwards of two months. They need good light, constant temperatures and adequate (but not excessive) watering. A conservatory is an ideal spot because generally it is away from the fumes of kitchen boilers and such like. If, however, you bring a miniature into a dark hallway you really cannot expect it to last long. The longest period I have ever had a miniature bloom in such a situation was two months, and that was very unusual. The variety was Little Linda, a creamy-yellow bloom that seems to need less light than many. A plant of Royal Ruby in the same situation did not do nearly as well and in a matter of weeks the buds were falling off and the leaves going yellow.

If you are thinking of having normal miniatures in the house the best way is to bring them in for short periods when they are fully in flower. Two weeks will be about the normal span, and then they should be put outside again. But if you can select the right place then there are many that will do well for longer. In the hallway of my house there is a table which the sun reaches for at least half the day, and there I have kept miniatures for quite a long time, especially the new Sunblaze series from the French firm of Meillands.

Feed the plants about every two weeks with a normal house-plant fertiliser during the season but don't expect to get year after year growth from the same plant in the same pot — you will have to repot them. Indeed, many that you buy will be almost rootbound and will need gentle easing into a larger pot and some new potting compost. Keep them watered; a plant that dries out is unlikely to survive. And watch out for insects — the biggest trouble in many indoor plants comes from white fly, but if you take the plants outdoors and spray them with a suitable insecticide you can catch the pest before it really causes trouble.

The best way to grow miniatures successfully indoors is in specially-created conditions, under lights. American rose growers are high in ingenuity when it comes to this particular art and I once saw dozens of miniature roses growing in a dark basement in New Jersey. It looked the most inhospitable and unlikely place to have perfect plants: but they were blooming marvellously well and completely out of season. And if a basement seems unlikely, what about the back of a cave deep in Kentucky? I saw them there too. In another place they were providing a perfect bottle garden, although it should be stressed that the bottle was a huge one that had been saved from one of the old drugstore displays. So if it can be done in places like these why don't more people have roses out of season? The reason is, I suppose, that it does require a little bit of patience, and work, to set the whole thing up.

The first rule of thumb is that you have to simulate summer outdoor conditions, that is with light, warmth and humidity, as well as feeding and watering. But before all that you must have your plants right. One enthusiast told me that he believes in bringing the plant on right from the start in indoor conditions; in other words, he takes cuttings from outdoor plants and roots them inside so that they live all their lives in the indoor environment. Other growers pot up the miniatures on their own roots — the smaller the better initially — and leave them to settle outdoors until they have spent a summer and a winter in the same pot. Then they are taken in and given their chance to provide out-of-season blooms under special conditions. Remember that many miniatures may well grow much taller indoors than they would in the garden so do choose the lower-growing ones to start with. You may find some nurserymen offering micro-minis: these will seldom grow too big and should be your main consideration.

The next move is to pick a spot where the temperature will not be too low. I tried some in a shed that was only a little warmer than outdoors and even though they had plenty of light they did not do well. But in a room where they have the benefit of temperatures around 15°C (60°F) at night and a little higher by day the story is different. This is the sort of temperature that exists in most homes these days; if temperatures fall to 4°C (40°F) or thereabouts the little roses will stand still.

It is possible to purchase commercial fixtures made for indoor gardening, and some of these are quite well arranged. But in others the lamps are nowhere near sufficient for miniature roses, no matter how effective they may be for other house plants. For growing under fluorescent lights you need a minimum of four 40-watt, broad spectrum tubes side by side, about 120cm (48in) long. They should be as close together as possible, not more than 8cm (3in) apart, and fixed so that they are no more than 10cm (4in) above the tops of the plants. If you are only supplementing normal light the distance can be greater. Look too for fluorescent tubes that are made specially for horticultural purposes.

If you are more ambitious you can grow roses on a small table where the fluorescent lights can be lowered until they are in the proper position. The situation will be improved if you can place the table against a white wall for more light. If this is not possible then a three-sided fixture can be constructed from white enamel, a white covered board or aluminium. The main thing to remember is that reflective surfaces above and behind the tray holding the plants will provide the all-over light that the plants need to succeed. Buy a switch timer to control the amount of light your roses will get; base it on the

32

length of light they would get in the summer, preferably about twelve hours of the day, although longer won't do any harm. Remember that under natural conditions the plants would have so many hours of darkness and that indoors they need their resting time too. If you regulate these hours to off-peak electricity times you will make quite a saving. This indoor light-garden need not be a giant construction. Think of it as something you can move whenever or wherever you want and all you will have to do is plug it into the mains.

The most important thing is to keep the temperature up to the 20°C (70°F) mark where possible. With a consistently high temperature you will get more growth and more bloom. But you will also have to do more watering, more fertilising and keep a watchful eye for insects. With lower temperatures the plant will grow more slowly and you won't get as many flowers, just as with a plant left in a part of the garden where it gets only limited amounts of sunshine. But you do have to water less and diseases don't seem to crowd in quite so quickly.

Another very important aspect of a healthy light-garden is correct watering. Heavy-handed watering can cause as much trouble as not giving enough. It is the same story with all plants — you have to know what they want and when they need help. Think of your own situation: on a warm day you need more water than on a cool day but even on a warm day you don't want to stand around with your feet in a cold puddle and your head burning in the sun. An even moisture is what is needed, and this applies to all roses in pots no matter where they are grown. The plant that wilts because it has been allowed to dry out has suffered a nasty shock and it takes more than a little help to get it back to its best again. Of course, the longer you leave it the worse it gets and the less are your chances of saving that plant. Water-logging is almost as bad, so don't drench your plants every twenty-four or even thirty-six hours. Your watering times will be dictated by the humidity, the temperature and, of course, the soil composition.

Much guesswork connected with watering and light can be taken out of indoor gardening by the use of moisture and light meters which are very simple to operate and do not need batteries or any other power. A miniature rose registering about figure six on an eight-digit water meter has about the correct moisture but you will need the light meter to give you the top rating for the miniature to be successful. A daily check with the water meter takes only seconds and will soon sort out the plants that are in need of attention. These devices are relatively inexpensive and are widely advertised in the gardening press.

The type of soil used for potting is your own choice. A widely accepted mixture consists of one part perlite, one part vermiculite and one part peat. The main trouble with this is that it is very light and makes plastic pots easy to knock over, though by the same token they are easy to handle. Peat alone, or with added nutrients or a peat potting compost, is useful but the main problem is drying out, whereas the problem with a sand-and-peat-based compost is that it is very easy to over-water. So the type of potting mix you use eventually dictates how you should water.

My own choice is a mix of all of these: peat, vermiculite, perlite and some soil pellets to give added weight. It is, of course, supplemented by one of the soilless fertilising additives. You will have to make sure that the roses are fed regularly with a fertiliser after potting — here I use a normal commercial mix. As these vary enormously it is impossible to give a list, but look for one that has been formulated specifically for roses.

Make sure initially that the plant is watered into its pot adequately. Fill the pot to the rim with water and leave it to soak right through. Then if you think that isn't enough give it a second soaking and leave it somewhere to drain, before placing it in your light-stand. Fertilise little and often; that way you can see how the plant is behaving and if it is in need of special attention. Use the fertiliser when the plants are growing well, ease off towards the end of their flowering span and don't feed until they start to make growth again. If a plant looks unhealthy or unhappy take it easy with the fertiliser.

One thing your miniatures will not survive is a dry atmosphere (probably the only plants that will are cacti). The air must be moist. There is no doubt that many plants fail simply because central heating or air conditioning has dried up the atmosphere. But it is possible even in these conditions to create the necessary humidity; some air conditioning systems have humidification added, but air can always be made more moist by the placing of humidifiers on radiators or close to the plants.

Certainly the best method with miniatures is to create a micro–climate around the bushes in their own stand. Place the pots over trays of water or above a gravel surface which is kept constantly moist. Don't allow the plants to stand directly on the gravel as this will only encourage the roots to start growing into it; lift them above it by placing them on inverted saucers. If gravel doesn't appeal to you perlite can be used instead, but this seems to dry out quicker than the gravel. Alternatively, you can cover a water-filled plant tray with wire netting or a wire grid and place the plants above the water, making sure that the tray is always kept topped up. Yet another method is to plunge the pots into a larger pot containing peat or perlite but again the problem here is that the roots will come out from the main pot and begin to grow in the outside mixture. Miniatures enjoy being sprayed occasionally by a fine mist of water, which will increase humidity and wash the foliage, but constant misting can produce disease and fungus problems.

Group the plants fairly closely together and they will help one another to create the correct atmosphere. If you feel that the air is too static a small fan will help. But have it blowing away from the miniatures.

Even after creating the most congenial environment you cannot expect your plants to last forever. They need the same resting time as a garden plant, ie about three to four months. Just take them from the indoor garden and leave them outside in some sheltered spot. But do not let them dry out, even in dormancy.

I have found that most of the varieties offered as micro-minis are very good in this situation. Little Linda is a particularly suitable subject, and Littlest Angel, with more yellow blooms is another. My own favourites, selected mainly because of their ability to produce a lot of blooms without too much bother, would include Woman's Own (pink), Bambino (rose pink), Lavender Lace, Green Ice, Cinderella (white tinged with pink), Perla de Montserrat, Sunblaze or the new range of Rosamini and Minimo varieties from de Ruiter.

It doesn't take too much imagination to understand why this variety was called Popcorn. It makes a superb garden plant and is smothered all year round with bundles of tiny blooms. (*McCann*)

34

5

PLANTING

To get good blooms on a miniature rose you must start off with a good plant. But even the sturdiest plant will fail if the soil is wrong. The trouble with soil is that you really cannot tell by looking at it whether it is good or bad; however, there are few soils that cannot be improved by preparation and fertilising.

The miniature rose is small and tough, but there is no excuse for not giving it a perfect planting. It is essential that you get the soil ready in plenty of time. The ideal is to dig over the garden two to three months before the arrival of the plants, but this is rarely practicable as there is always some other job that needs doing and the digging is left to the last moment. The earlier the preparation the better, however, as it gives the soil a chance to settle down and to absorb the nutrients, ready to feed the roots of the miniature when it is planted.

For garden or for exhibition, Rosy Dawn is likely to become a favourite. Raised by Dee Bennett in California, it is a vigorous, well branched bush that grows up to 24in (60cm) tall. (*Tiny Petals Nursery*)

Orange Honey, a rose that does very well the world over. Tiny and perfect, it grows into a good bush – though the blooms lose the pure orange colouring as they fade. (*R. S. Moore*)

Good drainage is essential for good rose cultivation — despite many suggestions that roses do better in heavy ground this is not so. Roses, and especially miniatures, do well in good ground and the better the soil the better the result. Gardens with heavy clay or other sticky soils generally suffer from poor drainage while sandy or stony soil usually drains well. If you want to test your garden's drainage dig a hole about 60cm (2ft) deep and fill it with water. If the water drains away in a day the drainage is all right but if it holds on for longer then you must do something to improve the situation. You can dig a long trench that will drain the water away to another end of your garden; this ditch will need to be filled with cavity blocks or large stones, so it is a job only for the fit and the enthusiast! On a smaller scale, by improving the texture of the soil with garden compost, leaf mould, peat or manure you can improve the drainage because in heavy soil the particles stick together and do not allow water through. There are chemical preparations available but the soil, in my opinion, improves beyond recognition with a little regular attention and the application of the organic composts.

The best time to plant miniatures really depends on where you live. In

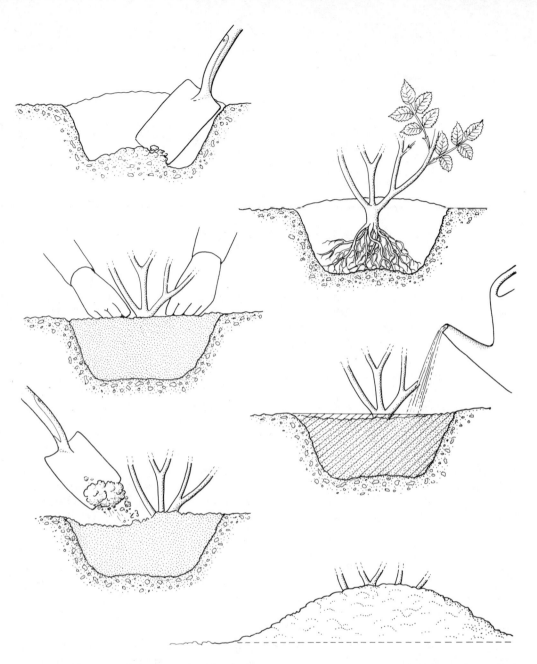

Dig a hole that will keep the budded or grafted point just below the soil level. Plant firmly but not, please, with a heavy boot. Strong fist pressure will do. Water in and then top up with more soil when the plant area has settled. Mound up if winter protection is needed in your area.

moderate climates it can be any time from midwinter to late spring, but in places where the temperatures go down below 20°C (−10°F) spring is best.

Frequently, miniatures will be delivered when, for one reason or another, you cannot get into the garden immediately. If the plants are own-rooted (and very likely therefore to be received in a container with soil) there is little trouble. You just put them aside in a sheltered spot until the time is right for planting. They will go on growing happily in their pots. But if you get bare-root plants, which are still grown in many parts of the world, then it is a different matter.

First of all keep them in the bags provided by the grower; you will find that the plants will happily survive a week or so if they are not disturbed. But keep them in a cool place; a heated room will be the death of them. By far the best way to tackle the problem is to heel them in temporarily somewhere in the garden until conditions are right for planting.

Roses that have been through the packaging and delivery service (no matter how good) will often have stems broken and others cracked or torn. If this has happened, cut away any damaged or broken wood and prune to a healthy bud below the damage.

Do not let plants dry out; it is better to leave them in a bucket of water in a cool place out of frost for a few days. And do make sure that before you plant them you give the roots a good soaking.

The best soil for miniatures is a good medium loam that never gets too dry and never gets waterlogged; if your garden falls short in this respect you must go as far towards creating ideal conditions as possible. The perfect pH (acid/alkali) balance is said to be 6:5 and this may be corrected with various additions — peat to increase acidity, nitrochalk to increase alkalinity. There are various little meters that will tell you the pH value of your soil and you can also buy small, easy-to-use kits for the same purpose. But probably the finest thing you can use in your garden is humus, in particular manure. (Beware of mushroom compost which really isn't suitable.) Best by far is well-rotted farmyard manure: horse (though see page 47 for possible drawbacks), cow, sheep or even chicken. Unfortunately this is not always easily obtainable nowadays, so you may have to turn to the more accessible peat. This is a useful addition which helps to hold moisture in soil that is thin or sandy and it also helps break down heavy clay soils, but it has no food value whatsoever, so if you use peat, add a commercial fertiliser.

If your garden has heavy soil then you must put the work into the digging. Double digging will probably be necessary. This means taking off the first spade level, then digging the next level as well and at the same time incorporating manure or peat as well as bone meal, hoof and horn meal, fish meal or meat and bone meal, all of which supply nitrogen, phosphorus, potassium, calcium and magnesium. If your soil is naturally light the top spit will be deep enough to dig because the rose roots will certainly find their own way quickly enough where the conditions are generous.

For planting I like to make up a planting mixture in a light wheelbarrow, using a bucket of soil, a bucket of granulated peat and a handful of rose fertiliser mixed thoroughly together and dampened. You should carry the roses to the prepared holes with the roots wrapped in a piece of sacking or suchlike; don't take them down the garden and leave them lying on the ground to dry out while you dig.

Always dig a generous hole, not just a long narrow gap; go at least 30cm (12in) across and down. Then you can be sure that there will be enough room for the roots to do well. Of course, it again all depends on the size of the plant and the length of the roots. I am not a believer in cutting roots — after all, the rose has spent all its energy up

Planting out potted miniatures is simple enough, provided the area has been thoroughly prepared. Water the pots well and then gently tip the rose out, keeping the soil ball together.

Loosen the bottom roots slightly and place in the prepared hole. Water in again and, when the soil has settled, add more to level off the bed.

to now in growing them so why come along and cut them off?

A miniature that has been pot grown will need more delicate handling than a bare-root type. If it is in a plastic pot you can take a planting choice. Water the plant adequately first and then cut underneath the pot with a sharp knife (if it is cuttable). Hold it tightly and place it in the hole. Then cut down one side. You will find that the two pieces of plastic come away without disturbing the roots. If the pot is not cuttable then don't water but knock the plant out and loosen the bottom roots just a little to give them a good start. Spread the roots out as best you can in the hole, cover them with handfuls of the planting mixture and then fill in. Make sure that you don't leave gaps that can hold water later on. Gently settle the plant in, don't trample the soil with heavy boots, and water it well.

Bare-root roses should be planted to the bud union (where the root and the top growth meet) while the potted (or own-root) types should be put into soil just deep enough to cover the roots. If you live in a very cold part of the world where winter and spring cover is needed you will have to mound the soil up around the canes or use one of the polystyrene rose plant covers that are generally available in these areas.

The whole idea is to create a hospitable home for your new plant. Good drainage, good soil and a good plant, gently eased into its new position and then watered in, will make the perfect plant in very little time.

The watering is important. It often happens that early spring can be a cold, dry season and that is when plants suffer most. Give them some shelter from the wind if you can — but don't keep them too sheltered from the watering can. Give them enough, not too little and not too much. A water meter will again help.

There are a few other planting tips that should not be ignored.

Do not plant new roses where others have grown, at least not unless the soil has rested from roses for about three years. The scientific reason for this is that the soil suffers rose sickness — a term used to cover something that no one seems to know a great deal about. In fact what happens is that if you dig up an old bush and replace it with a new one you will find that the new one will not thrive although the old one, if left alone, would continue to do quite well. The old rose roots have obviously gone beyond the worn-out soil and are thriving, whereas the new roots can't manage in the tainted soil. You have to excavate quite a large area and refill it with new soil if you want your new plants to settle in and get growing in the best conditions.

Much the same problem occurs when miniatures are planted along the front of borders where the older roses have grown too tall. Miniatures cannot be expected to do well in such conditions. Not only are they competing with older, more mature roots for the goodness of the soil but the soil into which they have been planted is probably worn out already. If you want to plant miniatures at the foot of an already established border you must again be prepared to dig out as much of the soil as you can and replace it with a very good mixture. Of course, if you are starting a border there is nothing to stop you planting your miniatures at the same time as the other roses and you can be sure that they will do as well (often better) than the bigger roses.

In a rockery the soil has probably only grown other plants so there will be no danger of rose sickness, but very often in old rockeries the soil does become worn out quickly. The answer is to replace the soil in the pocket where you intend to plant the roses.

6

PRUNING

Pruning roses, whether they are miniatures, hybrid teas or climbers, is a subject so fraught with different methods that just to mention it can almost provoke another War of the Roses.

When is the right time to prune? That's one of the first controversial points, usually followed by arguments about the type of pruning: long, medium or short. Beginners can find themselves left completely behind by the talk about outward-facing eyes, slanting cuts and whether one should spray and feed immediately after pruning. Mercifully, the pruning of miniatures is a relatively straightforward operation, although even here there are a number of different approaches.

First, there are the gardeners who say: 'Take the shears and trim them as if you were trimming a hedge.' They may even add: 'Go right to ground level.' Another school of pruning says: 'Prune them as you do the bigger roses', but then this immediately provokes the other arguments about long, medium and short pruning. There is even a third school that says you should treat every plant with meticulous care and have a reason for making every cut.

The garden-shears idea, which sounds by far the easiest, is one perpetuated mainly by the rose breeders.

Before mechanisation they used shears for lopping off over-long growth before they despatched roses to the public. It was all right for them, they were not going to have to grow the roses after that. And, of course, when miniatures came along with such abundant small growth, pruning became too overwhelming a task for the breeders to do anything other than take a bunch and lop them indiscriminately. I have also heard the shears theory put forward by a leading miniature grower in San Francisco, so it is a method that has some use. It might have its place if you had a big number of miniatures to prune but it falls down on a number of basic principles that must always be kept in mind:

● Pruning is really all about keeping the plant young; the better the pruning of an individual plant the longer the life that can be expected from it.
● Pruning should make the plant grow the way you want it to, not the way it is naturally inclined to go.
● Pruning means giving new life. You can't give new life to dead or damaged wood, so you must cut it out. If this is left behind by casual trimming it only encourages insects and disease.
● Pruning also means taking away the short spindly growth that will never

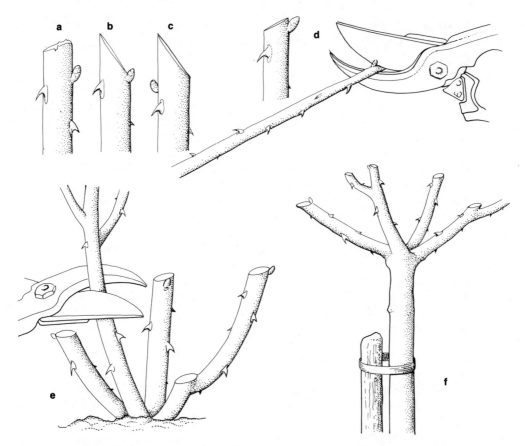

produce decent blooms. Again, without individual attention this can be missed and the plant has to do a huge amount of extra work to keep the weak stems alive.

So, pruning means making life easy for the plant to produce top-class blooms — lots of them. The hazards of light pruning, or no pruning at all, can be seen in gardens that have been allowed to run wild. The roses look like so many pieces of old wood, grey and gnarled, producing a minimum of blooms each year.

I look on pruning as the start of my rose season. Indeed, I probably get as much enjoyment out of doing it, as I do in looking at the roses in the summer. It is the promise of worthwhile results that counts.

I don't think there is really much

Pruning is just as important to miniatures as it is to any other type of rose. However, because the plant is smaller, it is harder to make the correct cuts. In the top left-hand corner are the wrong type of cuts: with secateurs that need sharpening or replacing (a); too close to the eye (b); and too far away from the eye (c). The correct cut is made with a sloping cut away from the eye about 3mm (¼in) above it (d). Trim bushes away to four or five strong shoots (e) and treat standard (or tree) miniatures in the same way (f).

doubt about when pruning should be done. More than likely your plants will have gone on producing blooms right into mid-winter, so early spring is the time to prune for normal summer flowering. Pick your own date and hope that it is a mild day without frost when you start the job. There is no need to worry though if there is a frost the following night; most miniatures will stand up to quite hard weather. If, of course, you are pruning for a special time, and intend to bring the bushes on under glass or artificial lights, then remember that it takes about ten to thirteen weeks after normal pruning for a bush to produce blooms.

One's first attempt can present its own problems. When the first spring came to my garden I had to call in a friend to help me, and she demonstrated so well that I have never looked back since. If you have someone close by who knows about pruning then don't be afraid to ask. In some towns (especially throughout the USA) there are rose consultants, members of the national rose societies, who will willingly help; and most societies carry out pruning demonstrations to show what should be done. Look in on one of these and you will find that pruning is in the end a simple, though vital, operation, and that much of it is just common sense.

To start with, you must get yourself kitted out. Miniatures are much easier to prune than bigger roses but they still in many cases have prickles and thorns that can do damage. So have a good pair of gloves and make sure that your wrists are covered too.

The most important item of all is a good pair of secateurs. Some people use smaller ones for miniatures but I find the normal 'parrot-bill' type, garden size, works well for me. The anvil type won't go between branches to cut out dead wood. If you buy good

secateurs they will last you a lifetime; don't let the initial cost put you off. You also need a kneeling pad if the miniatures are planted out in the garden. Of course, if you are lucky enough to have them all in pots the job is so much easier. You can sit down and make a work of art of the pruning.

Basically the same rules apply to pruning whether the bush is in a pot or in the ground.

Look at your miniature and you may find, especially if it is a modern variety, that it sends up a thick shoot that carries blooms candelabra style in the summer but that there are no breaks or eyes for a long way down this stem. The temptation is to just trim around the top of this stem. Don't, because it will grow very high, carry even more thin, unproductive wood and give you a plant that is very much out of balance. Cut it back to a good eye, facing outwards — an eye is a dormant bud found in the leaf axil. Look down the stem and you will see little nipples starting to grow. Pick one that looks pinkish and ready to burst into life and make a slantwise cut 6mm (1/4in) above it. (The angle of the cut is not, in fact, all that important with miniatures, many of which have stems that are too thin for such precision.) Try to find an eye pointing out from the centre of the bush. If you leave one pointing to the centre it will just get misplaced in a confused bush. The general idea is to keep the centre of the bush as clear as you possibly can. If you have difficulty finding one of these elusive 'outward-facing eyes' don't let it worry you. Just cut where you think there may be one and when growth starts you can always cut again more precisely. If growth happens to be going in the wrong direction then cut back still further to the next eye. There are one or two sprawling types, such as Stacey Sue, that are best pruned to inward-facing eyes when grown as a bush or standard.

The next step is to look out for small, thin wood near the base of the plant and cut it hard back. There is also likely to be some brown, old wood, the stumps of previous pruning that were not cut away. Cut them out as close to the base as possible. Always cut away frosted stems to clean wood where the pith is not browned.

When you are working on a plant, prune one bush at a time and do the job completely. Take away any bits of leaves or other rubbish that may have gathered there. If you have a budded plant clean the area around the bud union — the thick nut-like lump between the roots and the new growth. This will give the plant an opportunity to send up new shoots.

Finally, gently scuffle the soil around the bush and give a light feeding of rose fertiliser, ie about 55g per square metre (2oz/sq yd). Then get your spray can and give a dripping spray of a combined insecticide and fungicide.

After that just sit back and enjoy the spring, and the beautiful blooms that will come because of the attention you have rightly given to your bushes.

7

FEEDING, WATERING
AND WINTER CARE

Time and time again I have heard people say that miniature roses should not be fed. The reason they give is that the plant becomes big, ugly and untidy — gross is probably the best word to cover their description. Nothing could be further from the truth. Miniatures need feeding as much as other roses, or any plant for that matter; they do not grow gross from proper feeding.

Yet sometimes a miniature rose is seen to be growing almost as big as a floribunda. The main reason is that the plant has been budded or grafted and the added power from the much bigger roots does make for a much bigger bush. The other reason is that the plant has been allowed to run wild instead of being pruned and cut back early in the spring. There is no reason why miniatures should not be allowed to grow big as long as the place they are planted takes a tallish plant. A good, lusty, budded miniature will produce many more blooms early in its life than, for instance, a small plant growing on its own roots. Eventually the own-root plant will catch up but initially the thrust will be from the budded plant.

In New Zealand, where roses do seem to grow bigger than anywhere else, I have seen miniature roses almost

as tall as a normal garden shed and carrying hundreds of perfectly formed and perfectly sized blooms. In many cases these were growing on their own roots and the flowers from them were good enough to win top prizes in the local shows.

So don't think of a miniature as being a little weedy plant. There was a time when the only miniatures that were available carried a few feeble blooms in the summer and then covered themselves with mildew. It wasn't a happy sight to see a rose like that and those earlier miniatures were not giving the value which they should have given. Had they been fed, sprayed and watered they could have been the toast of the town. Proof of this can be seen today where there are still bushes of early varieties such as Baby Masquerade and Little Buckaroo. The former grows in the municipal garden of Baden-Baden in Germany and it is a feast of gold, red and pink blooms all summer long, which can be put down to the fact that it gets correct feeding.

What is correct feeding? If the bush has been planted correctly in good soil with some fertiliser added before planting then in its first year it can happily go until after the first flush of bloom without anything added to the soil. But from then on the rose does need attention. The essentials to remember are: food; water; sun; air.

The roots of the miniature search the soil for both food and moisture and, while you don't want to encourage laziness, these simple needs should not be neglected. Roses need two types of fertiliser: a slow-acting one that is there when they want it and the other a fast-release and easy to digest food.

My annual feeding programme begins after pruning, when I clean up the bed, gently hoe the top soil and add a rose fertiliser. Then, whenever possible, I add manure as a mulch — although peat, bark or hops will do quite well. Look around locally for a good mulch. It may be that there is a brewery near you where you can get hops, or a sheep farm where you can get dags (the end of the clippings, a mixture of fleece and excreta). Beware, though, of many of the bark derivatives as they tend to eat the nitrogen from the soil quicker than any plant.

Spread the mulch over the ground and leave it to rot in. Do not dig it in otherwise the value as a weed preventative will be lost — and you will also cause all sorts of damage to established roots by digging around the bushes.

I have found getting manure troublesome and on some occasions I have had to resort to the left-overs from horse stables. This looks fine because nowadays horses are often bedded down on either peat or wood shavings of different sorts. But there are problems. First the wood pulp must be watched in case the roses suffer from nitrogen deficiency (see Trouble-shooter's Guide page 57). Also you do get a lot of weeds growing through from undigested seeds in the droppings. A slight cut of the hoe will knock the weeds out of sight as they are only top rooted, but

No one can ever say that miniatures are dull – you can get almost every colour in the range. Here is Happy Hour, bright red in the bud, but with a bright yellow eye when fully open. It's a Harmon Saville rose.

if they get away from you the garden can look pretty tatty very quickly.

There is no doubt that a spring mulch is the key to success in the garden, especially if put down before new growth starts — later you can damage stems quite easily. Good old rotted cow or sheep manure is still the best, with peat a close second. I haven't tried hen litter but I visited one garden in the United States where there was a hen house at the top of the hill behind the garden and when the house was washed out the water ran down into the roses. The bushes along the edges of those beds were a sight to behold.

The most interesting mulch I have ever seen was in a carpet garden! The owner looked around for old carpets that had been dumped, especially those in browns or greens. He took them home, cut them into large pieces that were easy to handle and then made slits for the rose bushes to fit through. It was a complete success, if a bit tiresome. But think of the advantages. He had a fertiliser down and the carpet on top held the moisture very well for the plants. It also kept the very hot sun away from the roots. There were no weeds. The method also had advantages in helping to keep the garden clear of fallen leaves and petals — this enterprising gardener just took out the vacuum cleaner and hoovered up the debris. When he wanted to add more fertiliser he just lifted the edge of the carpet and scattered it underneath. The carpet did begin to look a bit rough and ragged after a year or so but he reckoned that he got up to five years from a good Axminster! The carpet generally cost him nothing and the maintenance rate was so low you wouldn't believe it. It was the best time-saver I have ever seen.

So a mulch is important whether it be manure, bark, peat or a carpet. And so too is the continued feeding of your roses. Apply a second fertiliser feed just before the blooms are formed and then again after the first flush so that the roses will go on flowering right through the summer and even up to late winter.

The important elements necessary for good growth are: nitrogen, phosphorus and potash. Nitrogen gives the growth and if a plant doesn't get enough it won't grow, the foliage will lack lustre and the bush will look unhappy. But too much nitrogen can also cause problems, mostly by producing lank and sappy growth that certainly looks wrong on a miniature. The object, then, is balanced feeding to provide a good, even-growing and eventually mature bush. When you get this you will have a plant that is much more able to withstand whatever diseases nature intends to pass its way.

You won't see the effects of phosphorus as quickly as you will see the effects of nitrogen on a miniature but it is essential to the rose's wellbeing and is vital if you want blooms that are earlier and look better. The roots also benefit.

Then there is potash, the hardening and ripening additive which makes sure that plants are in a good condition to meet the winter. Do not use muriate of potash — you want sulphate of potash.

You will get all these and various trace elements in the accepted rose fertilisers, which are much the same the world over and are as important to a rose in Hawaii as they are to one in Switzerland. Certainly I would still opt for a well-balanced commercially produced fertiliser; the difference in cost is minimal and you are not taking a gamble on the mix. Your miniature roses should get two or three applications of this a year, plus a dusting of sulphate of potash — not more than 55g per square metre (2oz/sq yd) — at the end of the summer.

Many people say that foliar feeding is unnecessary, but it certainly does no harm and when there is a drought it is of benefit to the plant. It reaches a rose quicker than the base fertiliser, though I would not use it instead of ground feeding. Foliar feeding is a supplement that I have found helpful and I use it in all sprays around the garden in the summer (see Chapter 8 on disease control).

The same fertilising rules apply to the growing of roses in tubs, pots or window-boxes, except that here you may have to provide a little more feeding. With the arrival of slow-release fertilisers the pot-growing techniques have changed radically in a few years. Now you just put one of the slow-release fertilisers into the soil mix and you don't have to worry for the rest of the season. But beware, don't use too much — it is not going to do the rose any good and it won't do your bank balance any good either.

A well-balanced potting mix is essential, plus an occasional liquid fertiliser; weak and often is my method. But in the container, as in the garden, if the initial soil isn't right you are wasting your time. One year I thought that these liquid feeds would make up for the lack of nutrients in a soilless compound and was rewarded by 500 plants dying while my back was turned.

The most important element in the successful raising of roses, wherever they are grown, is water. It is still the most overlooked essential in the rose garden and in dry weather miniatures will need a good deep watering every few days. A sprinkle on the top does more harm than good; the roots need soaking right down to the base especially when the weather is both dry and hot. This will be necessary with pots or tubs, where the soil dries out far quicker than in the ground. Peat especially is particularly vulnerable to this quick drying-out process and if it does dry out it is almost impossible to bring it back to good condition.

If you miss out a plant and it looks distressed, water it diligently until it is back to its best. If it is in a pot, soak the pot up over the top in water. I use a small baby's bath (a family heirloom) for this purpose. Once a month in the summer I soak the small pots in this bath — a tedious but necessary process. With a watering system laid on it would be a different story. Watering systems are not all that expensive these days. Certainly in the US the value of watering is understood and there I have seen some really expensive and spectacular systems. The most simple was a hose left along by the roses with holes put in it by a hot skewer; the water just bubbled out of these for an hour or so each day and the plants responded marvellously to it. Flat, perforated hoses which can be laid on beds and borders for the duration of the season (and to which automatic feeders can be attached) are readily available nowadays in most countries and save a lot of work.

When I feel that the roses need something quicker than the normal root feeding I often take a large barrel full of water, mix in some liquid feed and give each garden-planted miniature a full gallon or more to soak right to its roots. It does make a difference and you can see the results very quickly.

When it comes to winter care, I am lucky enough to live in a climate where I never need to do anything more than wish my roses a happy hibernation. But I have seen the efforts that some gardeners have to make to preserve their roses through really severe winters. It is generally true that many varieties of the miniature are tougher by far than their bigger counterparts but as more and more breeding is done it seems that winter hardiness could be lost to many.

What is too cold? If you live somewhere where the temperature goes below −7°C (20°F) for long periods then you will have to consider putting the woolly vest on the plants in open ground. Possibly in places such as the north of Scotland some miniatures would need watching, although I haven't met anyone who has had to resort to these methods in the United Kingdom or Ireland. What you have to watch out for is alternate freezing and thawing, and cold winds. Cold winter winds take the moisture from plants and nothing dies faster than a dried-out plant. So you have to keep the winds away and minimise the freezing/thawing/freezing routine.

Rosarians should not feel rushed

49

into covering up plants at the first signs of a cold snap but when the prospect is of a prolonged cold spell then that's the time to mound up the bushes with either soil (not hacked out from the surrounding area but additional to the site) or materials such as bark chippings, hops, sweet corn cobs or oak leaves. But the simplest protection must be the rose cone which is widely advertised in America. This is generally a styrofoam cap or bucket that is put over the rose and weighted on top with a brick to keep it from blowing away. You can also make a paper collar, stapling three or four thicknesses of newspaper together and then filling in with soil. I have also seen roofing material used the same way. Whatever you use make sure that any bud grafts are covered well; that way you will have plants in the spring.

Pots and similar small or relatively shallow containers need protection in either a greenhouse or a cold frame. At least make sure to put them under cover during periods of severe frosts because left out in the open they can freeze solid and the plant will be debilitated or die.

Where you are growing standards (tree roses) the crown must be protected in such cold periods too — indeed they are more likely to be killed than bushes. The old method of intertwining straw or hessian between the stems and tying under the crown is not much trouble and still quite effective. However, if you live in the parts of the world where the cold really hits hard you may well have to bury a standard rose to keep it alive for another year.

8

PESTS AND DISEASES

I once wrote that if I had a coat of arms it would probably be black spots on a rust-coloured background with aphid and caterpillar rampant. If you have a lot of roses there is no doubt that you will see these pests and diseases at some time among your plants, with a touch of mildew for good measure. But all the diseases and pests you could get on a miniature rose don't come together. In Britain and most of Europe the main rose problems are on a par with, say, a cold in the human head. After three days, with a little care, they can be banished. Not every part of the world is as lucky — there are places where spiders, mites, midges, raspberry cane borer, thrips, rose budworm and the disgusting Japanese beetle are individually rampant, though I have never met a gardener unfortunate enough to have the whole lot at one time!

If diseases or pests do, however, get a grip on your garden you can be in trouble. So remember the old adage that prevention is better than cure, and pay attention to detail. It is fortunate that miniatures today are probably the healthiest of all types of rose and a little care will go a long way to keeping them that way.

Anyone with a knowledge of the history of miniatures will tell you that their greatest problem in the past was mildew. Today mildew is far less likely to hit your miniatures than ever before and when it does you should look carefully at the situation and determine quickly where the fault lies. Miniatures, for instance, are likelier than big roses to be planted in some corner where the air doesn't get to them; and some of the reasons for mildew are poor circulation, a draughty corner or extremes in temperatures. A good mulch, as suggested in Chapter 7, is a great help. But if there is mildew on the miniatures and you cannot change their situation then a good spray programme is the next best thing.

The next big problem is likely to be black spot, and this unfortunately cannot be cut out by a change in the garden situation. Black spot has become far more common to gardeners everywhere as clean air programmes eliminate most of the industrial spillage that kept the disease at bay — it is sadly true that the cleaner the air the more black spot your miniatures are likely to get. The trouble, however, is that when you see the first black or brown spotting it is too late to save the leaf (despite what the chemists tell us). But it is never too late to save the rest of the bush and black spot is not fatal unless allowed to run riot year after year. The disease debilitates a plant by taking the foliage from it and there are few things as ugly as a beautiful miniature bloom sitting on top of a thin stem that has been completely denuded of leaves. It can be controlled with regular use of a systemic fungicide. Spray early in the season when the first leaflets begin to appear — catch them young and they will have in-built immunity. That way you can go far to beating the disease.

A third disease that I have found frequently among my miniatures is rust. Think of a piece of metal that has been allowed to lie outdoors in all weathers for some time and you will immediately know what rust looks like. I have seen some bushes so badly affected that I just had to shake the leaf for my hand to be coated in rust. It is less unsightly than either black spot or mildew but it is far more likely to kill off the plant eventually. There was a time when it was advised that the only way to overcome the disease was to dig up the plants and burn them. But fortunately science has come to our aid. The first and the most effective single spray against rust is Plantvax, although today there are a number of combination sprays that are geared to beat all three diseases — mildew, black spot and rust. If, however, you see the bright rust-red spots on the underside of a leaf get some spray immediately. It will save your plants.

These are the three diseases most likely to hit your miniatures, no matter where you live. There are some others that can be found in certain countries: crown gall and botrytis in the US, for instance, and some virus diseases in New Zealand. In most cases there will be a localised cure for these and miniatures have so far stayed quite clear of many of the less common virus diseases which can strike the larger roses.

The Trouble-shooter's Guide on pages 57–61 explains how to recognise and treat most of the troubles, including pests, that are likely to affect your roses. Knowing the warning signs and knowing the remedy will mean that half the battle has been won. It simply needs a regular watch on the plants. A great deal of my time in the summer is consumed walking around the miniatures looking at them. These walks are the most enjoyable part of the day and while I'm walking I may well spot a spittle bug or a greenfly and can take action. All the time I am looking at the little roses I am assessing how they are doing and how I can help them do even better.

The greatest help in avoiding diseases or pests is cleanliness in the garden followed by an early spray to catch the first bugs and then regular care. Pots and containers need special attention because there is always the possibility that some predator may get in among them.

For instance, for years my potted miniatures (and some big roses too) had their roots eaten away by a little nasty called a vine weevil. It gave me an impossible task of cleaning up every pot every year and replacing the soil completely. With 1,000 pots at times, it was such a problem that I was on the verge of giving up keeping potted plants of any sort when I found a gamma drench that cleaned the place in a couple of sprayings. I give this as an illustration of the frustrations that can sometimes overcome a gardener. In this case I failed to look for professional help which was there all the time.

Always ask for help — there is an expert around every corner. For

Here's what a really well grown pot rose should look like – plenty of bloom, clean foliage and good growth. This is Air France, which really only does well indoors (as intended), from Meillands of France. (*Meillands*)

instance, the American Rose Society nominates from each branch a consulting rosarian who is regarded as an expert in all forms of rose culture and who will be only too happy to come to your aid at any time. I have advocated this same system for the Royal National Rose Society in Britain. However, in Britain there are so many rose enthusiasts that it is generally very easy to find the local expert, and that is the person to ask. The amount of help and goodwill available throughout the world from rose societies is truly amazing with even the greatest experts sharing their secrets with the beginners. The point to remember is that you shouldn't be afraid to ask questions, however basic they may seem. When a rose expert comes along to talk in your town, go along with your list of problems and get value for your money. Asking about pest or disease control or cultivation is good sense because there may well be one local tip that can save your situation.

Looking at all the enemies of the rose one must be thankful for sprays that are insecticide, fungicide and even a foliar feed all combined. There was a time when I advocated everyone doing this for himself — mixing compatible fungicides and insecticides and foliar feed — but now commerce has taken the hard work out of it all. Used with discretion these sprays can effectively give you control in your garden right through the growing season.

One thing that should never be

Make Believe, a 1985 introduction from the master miniature breeder Ralph Moore. A vigorous grower with a larger than normal bloom. (*R. S. Moore*)

The Sunblaze roses introduced by Meillands have made quite an impact in Europe. They are ideal as short-stay houseplants or for window boxes or pots. Pictured here is the lovely white Yorkshire Sunblaze. (*Meillands*)

overlooked is the care and storing of your garden sprays. Find a dry cool part of a shed out of direct sunlight. Keep the various sprays apart; have a section for insecticides, another for fungicides and yet another for foliar and other fertilisers. Make sure that anything like weedkiller is kept out of the same area. It is so easy to pick up a container and, engrossed in something else, go ahead with your spraying and find that you have used a weedkiller. Keep all compounds in their original containers. This may need special care too, because if you leave them about in spaces under, say, greenhouse shelving you will soon find out that there are thousands of pests that seem to love the paper labels. So if the containers come with an outer covering use that; if not use a small plastic bag to cover them, which will give added security if a bottle should spill or a package break.

Care with the compounds themselves should also encourage care with the spraying equipment used. Clean it out thoroughly after every spraying and never use the same equipment for a weedkiller that you use for a pesticide or fungicide or anything else. Weedkiller traces remain after a long time.

Finally, don't leave any of the compounds or equipment around where they can be carelessly used, or taken in play by children. Even adults fall victim to the unlikeliest bottles and hospitals have rung me in the dead of night asking if I can identify a labelless bottle from which someone has drunk the liquid. Even when I can, the results are often fatal. So no matter how innocuous the spray you are using, keep it safely away and always put it back in its place. Never make up any spray in a container which is likely to be mistaken for a drink. Frequently it is the expert gardener who does this and then makes the fatal mistake of forgetting, and drinking the liquid.

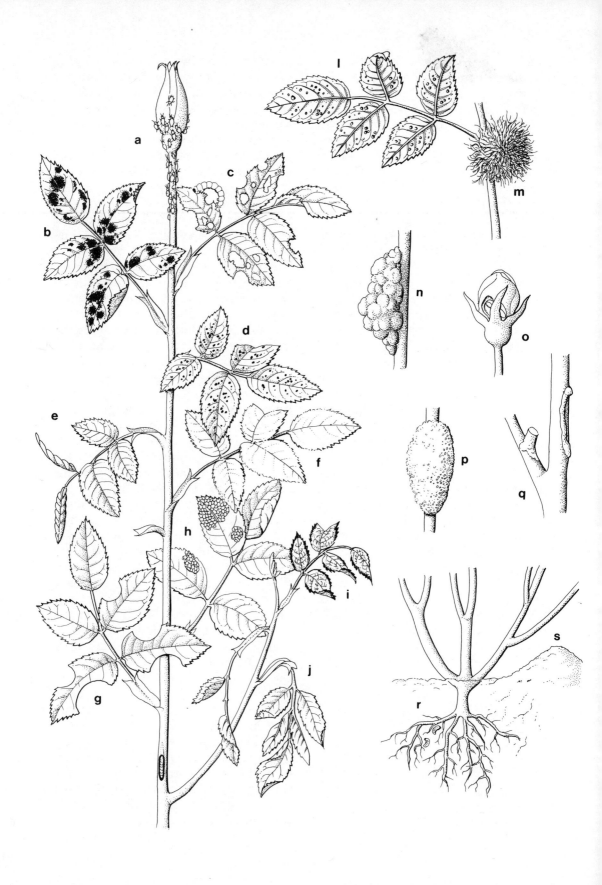

Trouble-shooter's Guide
Plants are slow to start

Check to see if they have been planted loosely; if the plant moves easily push the soil tighter around the neck. Wind rocking after planting will loosen bushes that may have been planted firmly earlier on. (If an older plant seems to be loose where it has been well established, look for a bug at the roots. It could be ants, chafer grubs or a vine weevil.)

Other likely causes of slow starting are: a waterlogged site, which is as bad as a site that is too dry — the roots cannot survive; use of fresh manure at planting time — manure should be allowed to sit for a few months at least and even then should be kept away from direct contact with the roots; dry roots at planting time — always soak new bushes for twenty-four hours before planting and then puddle them in. If there is a spell of dry weather after planting be sure that the miniatures are carefully monitored for their water needs.

If the cause does not appear to lie in the plant's situation check for weevils. This is an unusual problem to find among roses but one that is particularly devastating if allowed to take hold. The vine weevil is about 10mm in length, creamy-white with a little brown head. It does the same sort of damage as a chafer grub or a brown weevil, and all three of these ugly, slow-moving creatures look very similar.

Weevils and chafer grubs multiply very quickly. In the open garden spraying or dusting with a suitable insecticide should be done in midsummer but in the greenhouse the likelihood is that from mid-winter onwards these pests are hard at work and can be found at all stages of development — eggs, larvae and adults. Soil should be sterilised before repotting and this can be done in a number of ways. The most accepted way is to steam clean it (you can buy special containers that operate on electrical current). Another method is to pour boiling water right through the soil, but if you have a lot of soil you need a lot of water to maintain the heat all the way through. There are also soil fumigants that can be purchased but these should be used with the greatest of care.

Once you have been bothered by these nasties then you must keep a very watchful eye out for reinfestation. Be extra careful of potted plants bought in. Since my first problems with weevils I now repot every new plant when I receive it. During the summer I give all plants a gamma drench, just to make sure. I have talked to many nurserymen about this problem and I find that they tend to laugh about it — but then they generally have very adequate facilities for sterilising soil. Of course there is always the possibility that plants can get the bug after they have been potted up in the best of soil. Polyanthas and primulas are frequently visited by the summer fly that lays the eggs so if you have miniature roses growing near these plants do keep an extra special watch.

Pests and problems. They look pretty frightening when assembled together like this but thankfully you don't get them all together! And they are all quite easily controlled by a little regular care. (a) Aphid; (b) black spot; (c) caterpillar damage; (d) purple spotting; (e) sawfly (rolling the leaves); (f) white coating of mildew; (g) leaf cutter bee damage; (h) slug worm signs; (i) frost damage; (j) die back; (k) another sawfly – this one gets into the stem; (l) rust, seen under the leaves as orange spots; (m) Robin's pincushion; (n) crown gall; (o) bud eaten by chafer bettle; (p) cuckoo spit hides a little green pest; (q) canker on the stem; (r) weevils at the root will cause devastation to any crop; (s) anthill.

Leggy plants with few blooms

They haven't been getting enough sun

or possibly enough food. Check for sunny position; they need six hours sun a day if possible. If the problem is lack of feeding give root feeding with a special rose fertiliser and also give additional foliar feeding. Small doses are better than a banquet.

Buds fail to open or fall off before they reach colour stage
Something you can't really do a lot about as the weather is nearly always the cause, particularly cool nights, little sun and cold winds. Heavy rain often makes buds water sodden and they go into a brown mess. It is best to cut blooms early in wet weather and enjoy them indoors. It also gives the plant a chance to set about producing a new set of blooms quickly.

But do make sure that there isn't an attack of aphids around the site because they too can cause all sorts of problems on the blooms as well as the stems. (Aphids are dealt with specifically on page 59.) Thrips can also be a problem — these are sucking insects and they love a bloom that is just about to open, usually one you have planned on being a winner! Brown marks, stains and distortions around the petal edges are indications. The normal garden insecticide doesn't work here and you will have to name your pest specifically when you visit a garden centre to get a deterrent. One thing in favour of the miniatures is that thrips seem to take to the blooms on bigger roses far quicker.

The presence of the rose midge can also cause blooms to be distorted or not to open, and both buds and leaves to turn black and die. The midge is a tiny brown or red insect that lays its eggs on the rose where the grubs can feed on the buds and leaves. While it is again more serious on larger roses than on miniatures it will attack if given half a chance. Spray once a week but if the buds have become too infected for a spray to do any good it is best to cut the bloom off and let the bush get on with producing some more.

Mottled, yellow, tinted or badly coloured foliage
Don't panic — if the plant is well and healthy looking it may be that light colourings are just part of its make-up. But when lack of colour appears with stunted leaves that fall easily, accompanied by an unhappy bush, then you know you have problems. Yellowing of the leaves, especially the young ones, denotes an iron shortage, too much lime, an excess of phosphoric acid or manganese, too much moisture, or damage to the root system. Avoid overliming, use a chelate of iron such as Sequestrene and then follow some days later with a foliar spray. All other problems such as nitrogen deficiency (small pale-green leaves, often with red spots, early leaf-fall), potash shortage (usually seen on sandy soils when blooms come small and foliage has brown, brittle margins) and phosphate shortage (stunted plants, small leaves and purplish tints) can be cured by the application of a well-balanced rose fertiliser used according to the manufacturer's instructions.

Leaves, stalks and stems distorted and dying off
Could be weedkiller damage, often the result of a lawn weedkiller or similar spray drifting in over the miniatures which are more liable to damage than other roses as they are closer to the ground. Cut off the affected parts and the plant should quickly begin to recover. Remember that a container used for weedkiller should never be used for any other watering operation.

White, green, red or brown insects invading the stems and buds
These are aphids, probably the most

persistent of all pests. They suck the tenderest part of the rose, taking away all the nourishment. They also increase a hundredfold overnight and lay as many eggs again. Definitely a pest to clear away quickly. There are two sorts of insecticides — one a contact spray that kills off the adult aphid, the other a systemic spray that goes into the plant, kills off the adults and stays long enough in the plant to kill off the next generations too. Some brands contain both contact and systemic and are particularly useful in halting a sudden attack such as can build up on plants growing against a warm wall or fence. A sticky secretion or a white mass of little pieces around a plant is also an indication that you have aphids somewhere about. Keeping a weather eye out for them will enable you to stay in control. If you object to the use of sprays and have only a few bushes the old-fashioned finger-and-thumb method will work, especially as on miniatures you are less likely to meet a large prickle as you run finger and thumb along the egg- and pest-strewn stem. A less gory method, often suggested as a variation to the ordinary spraying programme, is to wash affected stems with soap and water. Unfortunately, it doesn't work. It does knock the aphids off, but the little bugs recover after a minute or so and when they are sure that no other flood is coming their way they just shake themselves and start scrambling up the rose again! Maybe a few lie dead but they are the unlucky minority.

I once tried bringing in a big collection of ladybirds to control the aphids, which they did for a while. But as soon as their food was gone the ladybirds took wing and proceeded to do the work for my neighbours, and by the end of the summer there were very few ladybirds in the area — they had obviously winged off to pastures where the killing was better. But if you are a believer in their effectiveness don't let me stop you.

Chewed leaves or buds

The caterpillar — in many forms. Fortunately this is another visitor that mainly troubles the big roses and is not too keen on the little miniatures which fail to give the larvae adequate cover. Low-growing floribundas, where the leaves are a great deal bigger than on miniatures, are also liable to attack. Watch for rolled up leaves and then pick off individual pests.

Leaves spotted grey, brown, red or yellow; leaf fall

Don't mistake this for black spot. It is likely to be red spider mite, a tiny spider-like sucking insect that comes when the weather is hot and humid and keeps out of sight on the underside of the leaves. A keen eye will know when it's there. It is a very serious pest in greenhouses. Spider mites have built up quite an immunity to many sprays so the gardener may have to try a number before finding one that is really effective. A fine jet with very good pressure is needed when spraying, which should be done every seven days to make sure that you clean away any new hatchings that emerge.

Large, circular holes in the leaves and blooms

This is the work of the Japanese beetle whose depredations are spreading across America and other parts of the world. It is the worst and the ugliest beetle of all. Look for a 1cm (½in) long body, metallic green with copper-brown wings. Hand pick any specimens from the plants and drop into a container of kerosene. My only knowledge of them has been in other people's gardens (along the east coast of the US) but I have seen the blooms turned over and the dreaded beetles falling out in tens.

White, frothy spittle on shoots
This is cuckoo spit or froghopper which appears early in the year. Leave it there and you will find distorted shoots. If you have only a few roses then the finger-and-thumb exercise of squashing the little greenish bug inside the spittle will be effective; if not, then a good insecticide used forcibly on the spittle will do the trick.

Regular-shaped holes at the sides of leaves
Caused by a bee called the leaf cutter. Control is not really necessary, the bee may be just passing by, but if the cutting becomes persistent then you must search out the nest and destroy it — ask a local beekeeper for help.

Skeletonised areas of foliage
Areas on the leaves turn grey or brown and all greenery seems to be eaten away leaving only the veins. This is the work of the rose slugworm — a greenish-yellow grub seen on the leaf surface. A systemic insecticide will do the trick.

Holes in the flower bud
Inside the hole you will probably find a small brown maggot known as the tortrix moth. If it isn't inside the bud look around for a curled-up leaf — and it will be in residence there. Pick off affected buds and you won't have trouble; but if the damage looks too much to cope with in this way you will have to buy one of the sprays that eliminate caterpillars as well as normal insects, and these are widely available in a variety of combinations.

Dark spots on leaves with a surrounding yellow area; leaves turning yellow and falling off
Black spot disease without a doubt.

Once almost unknown in industrial areas it is now to be found just about everywhere as the clean air laws are rigidly enforced. It starts as early as the first buds of spring and if allowed to keep going will give a plant with small undernourished blooms and no foliage. Spray with one of the many new and very effective systemic chemicals every ten to fourteen days and you will be on your way to winning the war. Pick off diseased leaves and keep a watchful eye for the starter spots. When the weather is wet and warm then you have the right situation for the disease to grow. A good idea is to alternate spraying materials.

White or grey powdery substance on leaves and stems; leaves curling up
This is mildew, the powdery variety, and the conditions that bring it on are cool nights, humid days and little rain. It is a summer trouble, just when you are not expecting such things to happen. Mildew is regarded by many as the most widespread of miniature diseases, though more and more resistant varieties of roses are arriving on the market. If your plants are susceptible then a look at where they are planted (too close to a wall where roots are dry and there is little ventilation, for instance) will often reveal all. A well fed and cared for plant will have a better chance of survival. Spray immediately the disease appears and if the soil is dry, water well. You will find that these days the same fungicide can control both black spot and mildew. So a regular walk with the sprayer is the way to success.

Rusty, orange-like swellings appearing at first under the leaf and then coming through the top surface
The old killer, rust, is seen early in summer and must be taken in hand immediately. A potash shortage

encourages the disease but adding that to the soil won't help if the disease is already there. The internationally available Plantvax is the real cure although, again, some sprays are being presented today that are quite effective against all three major diseases — rust, mildew and black spot. Don't always blame the rose; some gardens harbour pockets of rust that will affect varieties that would have remained healthy elsewhere.

Rough, tumour-like growths near the roots
These are caused by crown gall, a disease that enters wounds made by digging or hoeing. It won't cause a great deal of harm on stems but like every disease is better done away with. Cut off with a sharp knife and then treat the wound with a sealant. Also disinfect your secateurs or knife. If the galls appear on the roots then the problem is more serious and the likelihood is that

the whole plant will die off unless you are ruthless and take it up immediately and cut out the bad parts.

Brown or sunken area along the stem
The bark looks as though it has been cut away and a disease has broken through. It is known as canker and it is often caused by damage while gardening and also by bugs eating away at the outer bark. It grows and will eventually encircle the stem, killing all wood above it. This is one to watch for in garden-planted miniatures because the little ones can be so easily damaged while you are hoeing or working the soil around them. Care is the first method of prevention, but if the canker gets big you may as well cut it out and burn the affected wood. When such diseased areas are found in early spring prune to a good bud below. Also clean the secateurs in disinfectant before using again.

9

PROPAGATING YOUR OWN

There has, in the past five years, been a new attitude to miniatures from hybridisers everywhere. This attitude was summed up by top breeder Sam McGredy in New Zealand when he said: 'I want to have these little ones as easy to grow as geraniums — and for them to take the place of geraniums.'

This is a dream that is coming true. Most of the little roses you can buy today will take as easily as geranium cuttings and will grow in just as many places, but they have the advantage of not having to be renewed by new cuttings or plants for years. The ease of propagation of the miniature has been the answer. The plants that come on their own roots have a great advantage over the budded or grafted plants — because the roots are seldom much bigger than the tops of the plants (and often smaller) they can be grown almost anywhere. On budded plants the roots can be twice as long as the tops so that planting in a window-box or some other shallow container is impossible.

There are six ways of propagating roses: budding, grafting, cuttings, layering, tissue culture and seed sowing. But the two to interest those amateurs who wish to increase their own stock are budding and cuttings. Grafting requires special situations;

layering doesn't really work with miniatures; tissue culture, which is explained at the end of this chapter, is not a method for the amateur; and seed sowing is mainly for those interested in hybridising (see Chapter 10). So let's look at the ways you can make your own little plants — as many of them as you want.

The most productive way to increase miniatures is by cuttings. Anyone can do it; you don't need a greenhouse or any special tools and the success rate can be something in the region of 90 per cent which is, of course, far higher than you would get trying to root ordinary roses.

With cuttings you get new roses for nothing and with a constant succession of plants either growing on or ready for propagation, your hobby could even become a little business. One Californian lady's husband retired with the dream of starting a nursery for miniatures in a yard no bigger than a fair-sized garden (about ⅓ acre). Unfortunately he died just when he

Miniatures grow very easily from cuttings. Select a cutting that has carried a flower and either cut it (a) or take a heel slip (b). Trim off the bottom two sets of leaves (c). Dip the cutting in a rooting powder or gel (d) and then simply plant in a small pot (e) with a good cutting compost.

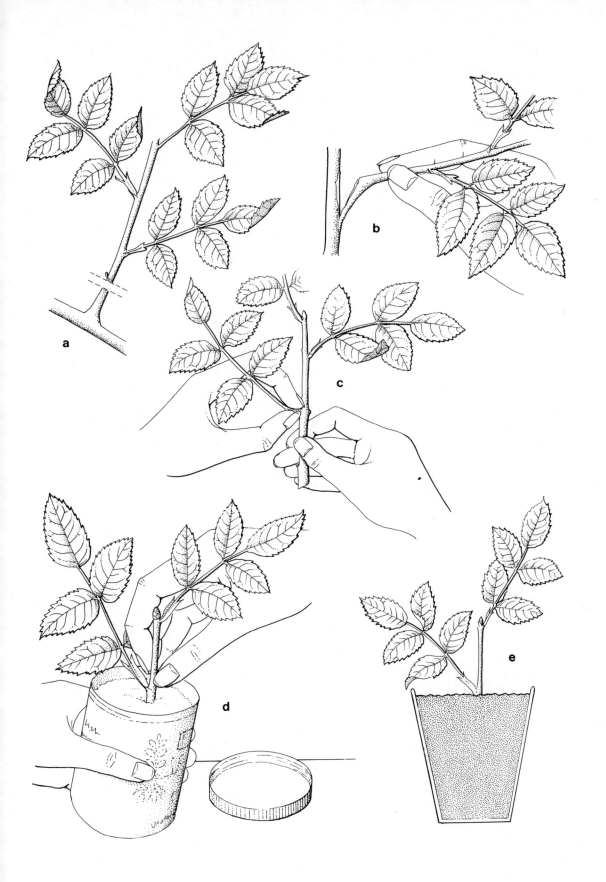

a

b

c

d

e

f

g

h

had the benches built and was ready to start. But his wife took up the challenge and made a great success of the business. She now grows about 20,000 miniature roses every year and sells them at local events. A vanload of small plants, most of them in bloom, will be sold in one day. The work isn't strenuous, apart from the van loading and unloading, which is only a small problem as the business gets going. This is not an isolated case — many of the smaller nurseries specialising in miniature roses in the United States were started this way by people who grew miniatures only as a hobby and then found that redundancy or retirement gave them an opportunity to start their business.

But anyone contemplating starting such a business should first consider the snags. To begin with, unless you live in a high sunshine area like Southern California, you will need a fairly large covered area with plenty of light and protection from rain and wind. There are other points to watch for too. For instance, you must have permission to propagate any rose that has been patented by its breeder and you will also have to pay a royalty on each plant sold. This is only fair when you realise that up to five or six years may have gone into perfecting that one variety, and in the process thousands of others will have been tried and found wanting; even the failures needed the breeder's time, money and know-how. However, there are a

Make sure that your cutting is kept moist (f) but not too wet. A small plastic bag tied over the cutting will provide a good home until the roots begin (g). When the plants have become established and the summer is approaching, they can be planted out (h) just like any other potted plant (see page 40). Otherwise they can be left to grow on in pots for a number years – all that is needed then is to change the pot size as the plants get older and bigger.

number of older varieties that were either never patented or on which the patent has expired. These can be propagated and sold without reference to anyone. Some of the 'free' varieties include Baby Masquerade (gold, red and pink blend), Beauty Secret (marvellous long-pointed buds of bright medium-red), Bonny (a deep pink from the German breeder, Kordes), Cinderella (dainty pearl-white), Scarlet Gem (orange-red), Mimi (pink) and Petite Folie (red blend), and there are many others that a simple search will reveal. It is not difficult to find out which varieties are patented: either the British Association of Rose Breeders, c/o 1 Bank Alley, Southwold, Suffolk IP18 6JD, or, in the US, the American Rose Society (see Appendix 2), will provide the answers. If you do not take this precaution then the hybridiser who owns the rights will quickly find you out. But there is nothing at all to stop you propagating any rose as long as you don't sell it. You may, of course, give plants to friends, and over the years I have found that a miniature rose makes the most satisfying of gifts.

One of the most important aspects of rose breeding these days is to find a variety that will grow easily from cuttings. You could have a super little rose but if it fails to take by the cutting method few nurseries want to know about it. So today it is almost impossible to find a modern miniature that isn't readily propagated by cuttings. At one stage in my life I had so many cuttings that I was giving them away by the trayful to visitors to my garden, though I did sell a few. I particularly fell in love with the number one American show variety, Peaches 'n' Cream, but found that it would not be marketed in the UK because British breeders reckoned it was too prone to disease and the bloom failed to open in wet weather. So I set out and eventually got a cutting which grew on for me. From this point it was simple to propagate and then I wrote to Edward Woolcock, the breeder, to tell him. He was delighted that I should get the bloom seen in England and so I sold about six of the plants. The rest I gave away. Very soon after distributing these I found the variety was winning top prizes in British shows. Like a lot of miniatures it does magnificently well in a cold greenhouse or in some other weather-proof area.

Getting a supply of cuttings is as easy as that. All you need is a finger-length shoot of the current year's growth that has become a little woody at the end. The theory was fairly general a few years ago that you could get a better take with a heel of the old wood, but this is really not necessary though many heel pieces of wood from a plant will provide two or more cuttings. In my own plantings I have found no difference between 'heel' cuttings and ordinary pieces of rose wood. All of them flowered well and grew into super little plants that would be a delight to anyone.

Take the cutting from a plant that has bloomed. It doesn't matter whether you plant the cutting in May or any other month up to October, your success rate will still be surprisingly high. Commercial growers of miniature roses say that it has been proven that cuttings taken from a plant that has been grown under greenhouse conditions (generally a cold greenhouse) will root far quicker than cuttings taken from a plant outside — but don't let that deter you. I have taken cuttings from miniatures growing in all sorts of situations and they have rooted well.

Short sturdy growths up to about 10cm (4in) long are what you want for the best plant. If you use twiggy little growths you will find that it takes ages for the rooted cutting to grow beyond the twiggy plant stage. Once you have taken the shoot off cut the base immediately below a set of leaves. Make sure that whatever you are using, whether it be razor blade (dangerous), knife, scissors or secateurs, the instrument is sharp, otherwise you will damage the growing 'eye'. Remove any flower that may still be on the cutting and also the bottom two sets of leaves, allowing about 2cm (¾in) for insertion in the soil. Plant immediately after cutting if at all possible — but don't let that worry you. I have successfully grown cuttings that had been left wrapped in damp paper for ten days.

Dip the end of the cutting into a rooting hormone powder (the commercial agent Transplantone is widely available), covering about the bottom 1cm (½in). Shake off excess powder, make a hole in the soil with a pencil, and plant, making sure that you have cut the end with a bud or eye at the bottom (see Figs 21a). Go away and leave it to get on with its own life.

Some growers leave the cuttings in a vitamin B solution but this is extravagant where the amateur rose grower is concerned and anyway I have never found it any better than the straightforward method described here. A countryman's recipe I once heard described is a very special way to aid rooting. The recipe is: take a bundle of pencil-thick willow branches 15–20cm (6–8in) long and soak in 45 litres (10gal) of water. Then soak the cuttings in this solution for twenty-four to forty-eight hours. Some people say it works and in the Vancouver Rose Society's bulletin, *Rose Bed*, the willow root-stimulant was highly praised.

The soil I use is a proprietary seed and cuttings mix. If this is not available mix equal parts sand and peat moss, but even straight peat moss will give you a good enough take. A normal seed tray will take about twenty cuttings. If you use the peat or peat/sand mix remember that the cutting is not getting any nourishment, so as soon as you know it has rooted (a gentle pull will tell you) pot it on in a ready-fertilised mix.

If you want to bring on only a few cuttings put two or three together in a small pot. Cover this with a plastic bag held off the cuttings with some taller sticks and make some holes in the bag to let in air.

Another very successful method with miniatures is to place the new cuttings directly into the parent plant's pot. The soil round a well-grown mini is usually excellent for bringing on cuttings and the parent plant's foliage initially protects the little plant from direct sunlight. Also the pot, by being kept regularly watered, provides a perfect life-style for the cutting. You also know immediately the identification of the new plant when it takes. It is a simple matter to ease out the rooted cutting gently with a small kitchen fork.

A recent innovation, the rooting bag, also works very well. You can put about fourteen cuttings into one of these small bags — they are heavy polythene filled with a well-balanced soil mix — and leave them outside if you want to. Just make sure that, as with all new cuttings, you keep them out of direct sunlight until growth has started and then gently ease them into the sun.

Most of the cuttings will be well rooted before winter begins but even so you must take them inside. They don't need heat unless you want to bring them on for special indoor display but do keep them away from heavy frosts and cold, cutting winds. A cold greenhouse in most climates is generally considered all right. If you

know frost is on the way protection with straw or newspaper should be considered.

You will find that taking cuttings is by far the best way of increasing your miniatures. Of course the new plants will take some time, say up to two seasons, to reach the size that you normally associate with budded plants. Don't let this worry you because the budded plant will take almost that long from the time you plant the stocks before you can begin to get enjoyment from it.

The time-consuming business of budding has almost been done away with by miniature rose breeders although some countries still continue to produce plants by this method. There is no doubt that budding (and grafting) initially produces bigger and stronger plants than those grown on their own roots but it is a back-breaking job when done in commercial quantities and no automation has been found yet that can compete with the human skill.

Budding is an easy skill to learn when you have only a few plants to cope with. Where it comes into its own with miniatures is in the production of small standards or tree roses. For these you must pot up good rose canes; you can buy some stock from most nurserymen or you can grow your own. When you have a suitable plant put it into a pot large enough to carry it for a year or thereabouts and do your budding in situ. Of course, you can plant your stock roots in the ground but this will involve the bending operation — in a pot, on a bench, the job is much less arduous.

Budding is a summertime occupation. Have your stock growing well in its pot (or ground site). Clear away the soil from the neck and wipe the stem with a clean cloth at the point where the budding is to be done — which for bushes should be as near to the roots as possible. If you bud higher up you will have a long-necked plant that is harder to manage later on.

The shoot from which the buds of the variety to be propagated are taken should be in prime condition and have carried a good bloom. When you cut the stem the leaves should also be cut off, leaving just a small portion at the end. The stem should immediately be placed in water and not allowed to dry out. The water should not cover the buds to be used, although these will dry out successfully very quickly. A good idea is to take the thorns away from the stem and if they come away easily then the stem is ready to bud. A special budding knife is useful but a short sharp vegetable knife will serve just as well.

Miss out the buds at the top of the stem, the best ones will be about half-way down. Cut away the lowest bud to be used first. Holding the stem firmly, make the cut about 1cm (½in) above the eye. Do not cut right through the stem but firmly and steadily pull away the bark. This should leave you with the shield that holds the eye. Trim it and take away any wood left behind the eye.

On the rootstock make a T-shaped cut, just long enough for the eye to be inserted. Open the bark and slide the eye through. Then the operation has to be sealed. You should be able to purchase some rubber ties from a local nurseryman but the old-fashioned method of wrapping raffia around the bud and rootstock is just as good. Soil up again to the base of the cut and let the plant get on with it. In the following spring the rootstock will begin to grow and the eye should be swollen and ready to burst through. If the rubber or raffia ties have not decayed, cut them carefully away and then head the plant back to just above the bud.

The plant will flower that summer.

The operation of budding is almost like that of pruning; once you see someone do it you will find it much easier to accomplish, so try and find someone to demonstrate it for you. Once you have mastered it you will be able to have strong plants budded at any height up the stem of the stock plant that you require. In other words if you require a normal bushy plant keep the eye as close to the roots as possible; if you desire a standard (or small tree) then place your bud at the height you want — 45cm (18in) is about right for miniatures.

A few years ago I was given a cutting from a small rambler and into each stem of this plant I put about a dozen eyes from the miniatures. When the eyes had taken the following summer I cut the stem into small pieces and found that it rooted extremely well. Later I tried the same process on ramblers such as The New Dawn and Albertine and again I found that the success rate was very high. In all cases it meant putting an eye from a miniature into the climber stem about every 20cm (8in) or so. You can do this with any rose that you know will root well and very soon you will have a number of well-growing budded plants.

The one thing you have to watch for when using budded plants is a sucker. You will know it by its growth — it looks very different from the rest of the leaves on the plant, usually being long and light coloured, and comes from below the bud union, which is the knobbly part just above where the roots are growing. Cut or pull suckers out as soon as you see them.

Without a doubt, tomorrow's way of raising miniatures on a large scale will be through the test tube and tissue culture plants. This will provide the most attractive commercial method of propagation, cutting out the long wait

68

experienced when budding, grafting or raising plants from cuttings. With tissue culture it is said that from a normal growing rose bush 10,000 seedlings can be raised in one year. In the traditional manner you might be lucky to get ten plants from a seedling in its first year by any of the other methods.

A tiny portion of the plant taken from between the shoot and the leaf provides the starting point. After impregnation in a chemical solution this tiny piece produces a small plant. This can again be split up into three or four or even more individual seedlings — all exactly the same as the parent plant. After this the whole business is speeded up and a complete crop of plants can be produced in one year. One of the first firms to try this with miniatures in Britain was Mattocks of Oxford, who launched the McGredy Benson and Hedges Special, a small yellow rose, in 1983.

At the moment this process is beyond the scope of an amateur but doubtless as more and more firms move into the area even amateurs will be able to use the services. If, for instance, someone breeds a miniature rose that they like, they will be able to send the plant away and designate the number of seedlings they want produced from that one specimen.

A rough idea of how important the whole area of tissue culture will be to the grower can be gauged by the fact that in Europe alone more than £15 million is spent on plants raised by this method. It has to be the greatest advance for decades as far as rose growers are concerned and certainly it will be the main area of plant production in the world of the miniatures.

Finally, there is another area of propagation — growing miniatures from seed. The raising of roses from your own grown seeds is discussed in Chapter 10 on hybridising but frequently 'miniature rose seeds' are offered in catalogues from general nurseries. These are not really seeds from miniature roses but come from the Fairy Rose, or *R. multiflora nana*, and the results will be disappointing in most cases. The seeds are very fertile but the plants they produce are seldom in the miniature class (though a couple of varieties that have won prizes throughout the world were a result of plants grown from these seeds). For fun, plant some of the seeds but don't expect too much. It is much better to do some hybridising yourself using the true miniature roses.

10

HYBRIDISING

I know of few things in this world that are as satisfying as breeding your own roses. It sounds an awesome undertaking and yet in practice it is one of the simplest tasks you can set out to do. I know, because I have bred hundreds. This doesn't put me in the same category as the professionals such as Moore, McGredy, Harkness, Warriner and the other famous names; but if I can do it, anyone can.

One of my children once put her finger on the pulse of rose breeding when she answered someone at the door who asked if I was in. 'Yes,' she said, 'he is down in the greenhouse playing at God.' I have never considered it in that category but at least it means that I am down there giving nature a helping hand.

Breeding a rose on your own isn't taking a slip or grafting or budding, it is finally getting a new rose from a seed. The stories you hear about the long process of getting a rose into the commercial market — in some cases ten years or more — have no significance in the case of the amateur. In fact, you can have a rose of your own twelve months or less after you make the first move. And by that I mean a rose that is different from anything else in the world — and a rose that is in flower! Amateur breeders have been

doing it very successfully for years now. At the moment Jim Jolley in England with Wee Barbie, Mark Spies in the USA with Cupcake and Eric Welsh in Australia with Wee Beth prove this point. Miniatures are proving themselves to be the easiest members of the rose family to breed from; they set seed easily and when you have your own little plant you can set about propagating more through cuttings. It might even go on to become a world beater — a number of amateurs have done just this with miniatures in recent times.

You set out on this wonderful game by having two roses that you like and crossing the pollen from one to the other, and vice versa, to begin the great task of creating a variety of your own. For many years I had been saying that I would love to do some hybridising and one day I found that my eldest son was doing what I had been saying. He had taken a bloom with a lot of pollen on it and scattered it on another rose which he thought looked good. The seeds did set and today some ten years

You won't have too much trouble getting Holy Toledo to produce blooms of a very good shape and pretty colouring. Like so many of the newer miniatures, Holy Toledo gets top marks for trouble-free growth. (*Armstrongs*)

later we still have one of the offspring of that cross and I still use it for breeding. But it could well be that if I hadn't had that initial push I might never have taken myself to the greenhouse and started breeding roses.

It truly is as easy as that. You put pollen from one rose on to another, allow the hips to set, and harvest them as soon as they show the first signs of ripening (an orange colour begins to seep into the dark green). Put the seeds away in a damp kitchen paper towel and leave them until late winter/early spring, when you plant them out in an ordinary seed compost. When the seedling emerges let it grow on until it gets too big for wherever the seed was planted, then pot it on and it will be flowering by summer.

That is the basic approach to breeding a rose. Of course the chance of it being better than its parents is a thousand to one and the chance of it ever being known beyond your own garden is greater still, but it is your own. It is unique, there is no other plant like it, and you can even put your name on it officially and have a rose that really belongs to the family.

If you don't want the trouble of pollination you can still go out into the garden and pick some hips that may have formed on blooms that were not dead-headed during the summer. You can use these to start, anyway. Take the seeds from the pod, give them the water test to check their fertility (those that sink are the ones to use) and see what happens.

But if all this has excited you enough I suggest that you start in a more detailed manner.

Stage one is parent selection and you must first of all find a miniature variety that readily sets seed. Two that are internationally available and which have been successful for me are Rise 'n' Shine (yellow) and Anytime (smoky vermilion).

You can get a good lesson in parent selection by looking up the work of the professionals. One name that will come through so many of them is Little Darling which isn't a miniature at all. It is a pretty floribunda that sets seed willingly and has been used so much today that there are few varieties that are not related to it somehow. Certainly much of the complicated breeding from Sam McGredy will show traces of this one which was never introduced into Europe because it tended to fall foul easily of mildew. Some breeders will show their faith in a variety in such a way that few varieties that they produce will be without it. One case in point is Ernest D. Williams, a leading US grower who uses Over the Rainbow very often and has had his faith rewarded by a succession of good varieties. Then there is Fairy Moss which was the starter for many of the moss miniatures that are available nowadays. But even with all this you will, I'm afraid, find that breeding a really good one is 1 per cent science and 99 per cent luck.

When you have chosen your parent plants, pot them up, let the plants settle well into the pots and then bring them into the greenhouse for use. If you are lucky enough to live in a particularly warm climate you can do your hybridising outside just as well as the rest of us do it indoors. Remember that you need both mother (seed-bearing) and

Joan Austin, a very good garden subject that produces lots and lots of bloom. The shell-pink on medium-pink colouring makes it an eye catcher. (*R. S. Moore*)

Creamy apricot is a colour that always attracts attention and, although this rose was only introduced in 1984, it has made a big impression on American shows with its flower perfection. It is called Jean Kenneally after a leading Californian rosarian. (*Dee Bennett, Tiny Petals*)

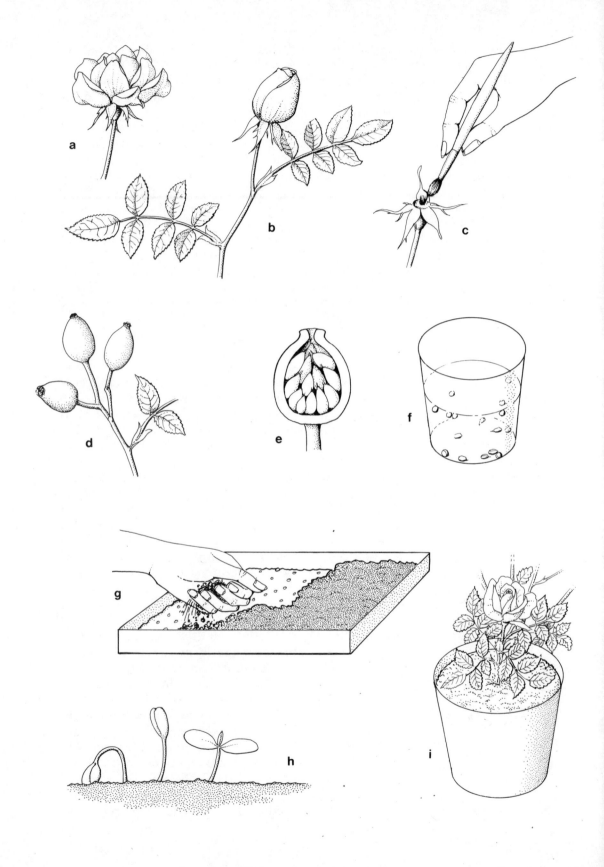

a

b

c

d

e

f

g

h

i

father (pollen-providing) plants, so the numbers of varieties and of plants required will depend on the number of crosses you wish to make, bearing in mind that pollen can be used from one to another and vice versa.

On a sunny summer's day prepare the seed parent. Select a half-open bloom and gently remove all the petals; make sure that you don't leave any ends behind. Then pick all the anthers off — either with small scissors or tweezers — and, if you are going to use their pollen for cross-fertilisation, let them drop on to a sheet of white paper, mark the name on the top of the sheet and put it aside (this is Sam McGredy's method and it is effective). Do the same on the plant chosen as male parent and the next day the pollen will be ready. How do you know? Just shake the sheet of paper and you will see the yellow pollen sticking to the paper. Using your index finger transfer the male parent's pollen to the stigma of the seed parent's flower. Some breeders use a brush but I find the finger method better. You can be sure your finger is clean of any pollen but you can't be as certain about a brush, and if the pollen gets mixed up your whole scheme of things could be upset.

At this stage many hybridisers wrap a paper bag around the bloom in case it should be visited by bees which might just pollinate it with another variety. I don't bother as I do it in the greenhouse where inquisitive bees or flies seldom enter. The pod begins to swell after a few weeks and slowly you see the start of your seed. A tip here: make sure that you tell any helpful neighbours or friends that they should not do you a favour and dead-head your roses when your back is turned! It did happen to me once.

After about twelve to fourteen weeks, depending on the weather, the hip will be ready for harvesting. Here again you will find that most hybridisers have their own method of working. Some breeders keep the hip whole until they are ready to sow the seed but I take the seeds out immediately and give them the water test by placing them all in a glass of water. Those that float are thrown out because they are usually infertile. The others are placed in a damp kitchen paper towel and then into a small plastic bag which is closed and labelled clearly with the name of the cross. Don't trust your memory — when it comes to the time for planting you will not remember which cross is which.

Many breeders say that you have to stratify — meaning after-ripen — the seeds and there are many ways of doing this. The accepted methods are: either put the seeds in small polythene bags with some damp peat moss and leave them in the fridge at about 5°C (41°F) for about six weeks; or just put the hips into the bags and take out the seeds later; or bury the hips in sharp sand and leave them outdoors where

Hybridising your own rose isn't as hard as you may think. Select the parents; the male (a) produces pollen, the female (b) from another variety stays on the bush to grow the seeds. Petals and pollen carrying anthers are stripped from the female bloom (c) just before the bloom opens, and pollen from the male anthers is brushed onto the female stigma. Seed hips should soon form from the female bloom (d) and the hips are left there until they begin to turn orange. A cut-open hip (e) reveals the seed. Give it the water test (f); those that sink are the fertile seeds. (It is virtually worthless planting the floaters, although some people do say they get results.)
Leave seeds in moist paper in plastic bags until January (about 8-10 weeks after the water test). Don't let them dry out. Plant them in trays (g) 25mm (1in) apart and about 6mm (¼in) deep. Seedlings will begin to show through (h) after as little as three weeks – or they can take up to two years. Transfer to a small pot and leave the plant to flower (i) in early summer.

the frost can get them (but the mice can't), again for about six weeks. For years I did stratify, then one year in exasperation I left the seeds in jam jars on the kitchen window and asked my wife to put some water in them occasionally in case they dried out. It was a busy summer that year and I did not look at the seeds until well into November. Then I was attracted to them because the papers looked so green. When I opened them most of the seeds had germinated. Since then I have never even considered any other method. Now I have something like an 80 per cent germination which I never had before and I don't have to remember to put the seeds in the fridge and take them out after six weeks. Do remember that the seeds must never dry out. As soon as you see some germinate in the paper, begin to plant all that batch.

I plant my seeds out in small ordinary seed trays. This is done fairly haphazardly because I am always short of time and there are usually about 3,000 seeds (a professional breeder will have anything between 50,000 and 100,000 or more). The purists say that they should be planted 1cm (½in) deep and 2.5cm (1in) apart; fine, if you have both the patience and the time. I plant them in as straight a row as possible with very little space between them. In anything from a week onwards some start to shoot through; they are very ordinary looking with two ear-like leaves, but when the first true rose leaf appears I take the little plant out and pot it on into a small pot. Peat pots or the grow-through pots are very successful here as the seedling can grow on and then be potted up into a bigger pot without any root disturbance.

The first flowers will appear in the early days of summer on a plant that is seldom much thicker than a matchstick and maybe 5–7cm (2–3in) high. This is the start of your very own miniature rose and also the time to make up your mind whether or not you want to keep the little plant. Some growers will throw out any plant they don't like immediately — a wastage of anything up to 80 per cent. I'm in the tender-hearted brigade and can't throw them out or burn them. I have generations of seedlings growing in the oddest places in my garden. The little ones that I can't find a home for are given to friends or taken into the countryside and trowelled into a ditch side somewhere. This is something that might be frowned on by farmers but so far I haven't found anyone who got annoyed.

Your miniatures can be grown on in pots for years or planted in the garden. If you want to give plants to your friends or send them to the world trial grounds you only have to take some cuttings and your new rose is multiplied. Should you decide that you have a plant that you would like to register, it is a simple matter. You get a form from your national rose society (see Appendix 2), fill it in and if the name hasn't already been used for a rose then it will be registered for you. If you want to find out what rose names have been used the best reference is an up-to-date copy of *Modern Roses*, a tome published by the American Rose Society that gives names and pedigrees of most commercially grown roses. But, again, your national rose society will be the body to contact — some of them will have computerised lists of the names of roses registered. Be warned, though, they don't like names that begin with Mrs, Miss or Mme, although I haven't heard anything said about Ms!

But what do you do with your rose if it is good enough? Amateurs have broken through very often and more so with miniatures than with the bigger roses. The first thing to remember is that growers who also breed their own varieties don't really want plants from other breeders so the secret is to look around for a nursery where the owner is searching for new varieties to add to his list. That isn't really as hard as it may seem provided you are prepared to let the grower have a small number of plants to try out under his own conditions.

For instance Tom and Jackie O'Neal, who run a very new miniature business, The Mini Farm in Bon Aqua, Tennessee, would come under this heading. In 1984 they invited me to send some of my miniatures for testing under their conditions and they added that if I knew of others who might be interested I could pass their names along. It is true that the major miniature growers are also breeders and therefore they offer fewer roses from other sources, locking out many good varieties. I like the O'Neal philosophy: 'We are not hung up on categories such as patio, miniflora or any other type

. . . if a rose is good the public wants it.'

The O'Neals aren't alone in wanting to promote new roses so the amateur breeder should have no excuses for not finding an outlet for something that is good. And if you want to show the world just how good your new rose is there are plenty of international rose trials where there are more and more opportunities for miniatures.

If you fail to find an outlet for your own rose through a grower then contact your national rose society who probably will be able to help. In Britain the British Association of Rose Breeders has always been willing to give guidance to amateurs with good varieties. You can get a great deal of practical help too from the amateur rose breeders' associations which exist in Britain, the United States and New Zealand. As the committee members of the bodies are amateurs the distribution addresses often change, so again the best way is to make contact through your national rose society (see Appendix 2).

11

EXHIBITING

If somebody asked me when my rose enthusiasm began I would have to say it was the day I entered a rose show. That was in 1969 and I went along with roses picked straight from the garden, not even hoping to win anything. But I did win and that was the immediate spur that sent me to another show the next week — and I won again!

Winning was nothing more than taking home a card marked 'First Prize'. The financial reward was something in the region of 20p, so it wasn't the money that kept me going, and it wasn't really the competition. It was the new dimension that it gave to my rose growing — the people were different, the excitement was great and the winning was fun too. One memorable day I swept the board at a show; every first prize card and trophy fell to me.

There were no miniatures at shows then. Indeed, at the Royal National Rose Society's Summer Show, the real show-piece of the British rose year, there wasn't much of a place for miniatures until 1975. Since then the entries in their classes have raced ahead every year. In the United States too the numbers of miniatures at shows have at many of the nationals outnumbered the other roses. And in New Zealand the reluctance of the hybrid tea and the

floribunda growers to take to miniatures is being broken down as more and more little roses arrive on the scene. Australia also reports that miniatures are taking a bigger spot at most shows while in Canada the prominence of the miniature is on a par with that in the United States.

Miniatures may indeed be the lifeblood of tomorrow's rose shows. It is widely acknowledged that the whole business of taking the big roses to the shows is fraught with fears, worries and nights without sleep. The blooms must be out days before; refrigerators are specially used for housing these by most American rose growers. The chance of having the rose right on the day is a worry that begins on pruning day! The true exhibitors will tell you, however, that this is what makes exhibiting so fascinating.

What a different scene it is with the miniatures. They are easy to transport, their holding power is phenomenal and they can travel thousands of miles with very little trouble. This is what makes them so popular at shows. The difference between taking twelve blooms of a hybrid tea and twelve blooms of a miniature from Teesside to London or San Diego to Boston, or from Auckland to Invercargill, is worlds apart.

If you grow miniature roses you can compete in your own town or village show, in the national show or even internationally. Indeed miniatures are practically the only type of rose which could figure in an international show because growers in England could still compete with those in New Zealand by growing the flowers out of season. It is an unlikely contest but the possibility is there. Certainly there is little to stop anyone in America taking a place in a British show, or vice versa.

Mr Frank Bowen, a former president of the World Federation of Rose Societies and an expert in growing miniatures, once said that the little roses were the perfect flowers to keep him in showing roses once the bigger ones got too much of a problem. The way he transported his miniatures was what made me take to them immediately. He made small holders for them which were placed inside a picnic box filled with dry ice. He could fit a great number of small flowers into the box and it was very easy to carry.

In the United States Dr Heber Eliot Rumble of Memphis, Tennessee, is a grower of some 500 miniature bushes and he also has an ingenious method of transportation which he has shared with members of the American Rose Society. His method is similar to Frank Bowen's, apart from the fact that the American rosarian uses the refrigerator much more than the British, cutting and storing entries for a show up to four days beforehand. Dr Rumble regularly enters something like 100 miniatures for shows in his area and is, of course, a major winner.

To copy his method you first of all need some 18cm (7in) round airtight plastic containers of the kind used to store food in refrigerators. Then make a trip to the local sports shop to buy some of the plastic tubes that golfers use for storing clubs. Cut these into

Classical exhibition form is shown here by Antique Rose, a rose-pink miniature from Ralph Moore. The variety also has something that exhibitors always ask for – good long straight stems on a plant that grows to about 46cm (18in) high.

short lengths (about five from the average golf tube) to fit the containers, you will find that about seventeen of these smaller tubes fit into one container. These will be used for individual blooms. For classes where sprays of blooms are called for, buy plastic water tubing of a larger diameter; about seven of these will fit into a container.

Dr Rumble cuts the blooms as they are ready in the garden, places them in warm water and grooms them before placing them in the tubes. The container already has a 50:50 mixture of water and a fizzy soft drink at the bottom. This is kept in the fridge at 1°–2°C (34°–35°F) and the tubes are filled as blooms become available, the container being kept closed tightly, of course, in the interval. When it is full he tapes the lid and does not open it until he arrives at the show. To remind him what is inside he tapes the names of the miniatures and their stage of development on the outside. He carries this individuality even further by placing the containers inside a large plastic bin containing ice. When travelling overnight to a show he uses an insulated bin.

One of the great problems about showing hybrid teas over the years has been the fact that the varieties likely to produce the winners on the show bench are also often the hardest to grow. They need more attention in every way and while this is one of the points that makes a winning exhibitor a true expert with these varieties, it also means that numbers of great roses fail to make it with the public because they are not seen at shows. This is not true with miniatures. I don't believe there is any variety of miniature that could not win a top award at a show. The leading show variety for a number of years, Starina, gets top marks for its growing habit as well. It is disease resistant, bright and carries a beautifully shaped bloom.

I always encourage people to exhibit their roses, not just to win prizes but to show the visitors the type of bloom that can be grown. The first thing is to find out when your local rose society show is taking place — do this through your local newspaper, town hall or horticultural adviser. Then ask the secretary if you can join the society (the fees are infinitesimal these days for the enjoyment received). That will get you a schedule straight away, but even if you are not a member few societies will turn you away. Check the schedule and decide where you are going to enter. There may well be novice classes and that's where you should start.

You really have nothing extra to do to the plants. If you follow the cultiva-

tion rules set down in earlier chapters, you will produce the goods on the day of the show. There are different approaches in most countries to the storing of blooms. Many people in Britain won't store them at all; in America it is considered a vital part of having enough blooms for the day. Many miniatures will keep up to a week in very good condition and that is far longer life than you can expect from a larger type bloom.

Good results can still be achieved without the preparation of special containers such as Heber Rumble's but you must keep your blooms in a cool place with water that does not freeze. Cut them just before they have reached the halfway open stage and you are unlikely to go wrong. A little practice with blooms that are ready before the show will give you all the guidance

(*Opposite*)
Gregory's of Nottingham were among the first British firms to show an interest in miniature roses, bringing in many of the top varieties, especially those bred by Ralph Moore. Here is a small selection: (*down left-hand side*) Beauty Secret, Little Flirt, Rosina, Baby Darling; (*down centre*) Easter Morning, Dwarf King, Scarlet Gem, Cinderella, Bambino; (*down right side*) Coralin, Baby Masquerade and Perle de Montseratt. (*Gregory's*)

(*Overleaf, left*)
Rainbow's End, likely to become a darling of rose exhibitors because of the perfection of the flower. It also has blooms enough to satisfy any gardener. When grown in the shade, blooms tend to be clear yellow but with a touch of sunshine it achieves the dazzling effect of red-orange tipping on the petals. (*Nor'East Roses*)

(*Overleaf, right*)
Stars'n'Stripes, introduced by Ralph Moore for the USA Bicentenary celebrations. This very unusual rose will be remembered more as a parent of a whole host of other striped miniatures. As a plant, its main fault is that it really doesn't produce enough blooms to make it a great garden subject – but for something to catch the eye this is the one. (*R. S. Moore*)

you need — there is nothing that beats practical experience.

If you are going to leave the bloom cutting until just before the show then you are taking a chance on having enough blooms, but miniatures are wonderful producers. I have often thought that I would have little or nothing for the next day's show but when I have gone to the garden the next morning the bushes have provided a very good collection of blooms.

Two days before the show water your plants well, not over the tops but right into the roots. On the evening before the show take a suitable container of lukewarm water into the garden and cut any blooms that are ready. Cut them longer than you think you will need with at least two, preferably three, sets of leaves. Place the roses quickly in the water. If some of the stems are thickish the certain way of getting the water through them is to cut them under the water. If you can cut the blooms at different stages of openness then you will have a range to choose from the next morning.

Do take some time to groom your blooms so that your work will be that much easier when you go to the show. Carefully remove all bugs or pieces of dirt. A small camel-hair brush is useful for this: a quick flick and the problem will be cast away. If something persists then take a piece of very soft cloth and wipe it off. With the same cloth take all spray residue and any other markings from the leaves. Do this very carefully — a thoughtless flick and you may well damage the bloom that might have been your top winner. Make sure that

Hotline, an appropriately named variety with classically shaped blooms that are usually borne one to a stem. Slightly mossed buds with a mossy fragrance. A new and reliable minature. (*Armstrongs*)

there are no scraps of cloth left about the rose. Once (and it hurts more and more each year as I remember it) I left a small piece of wool on a bloom that could have won a championship for me. The bloom was disqualified. A lesson learned the hard way.

Another point to watch is the naming of your roses. A wrong name on a bloom in a show can well be the difference between winning and losing; and although you may think you know the name well, when tomorrow comes there will be so much going on around you that you could easily forget that vital point.

Frank Bowen is very keen on presentation and he has this to say about it:

The presentation of your roses on the judging bench is vitally important and can make all the difference between winning and being just beaten — which is never good enough for any exhibitor. Presentation, which covers arrangement of multi-stem exhibits, such as vase and bowl classes common in Britain and elsewhere, carries points which not infrequently in fierce competition will determine the leading prizewinners. So present and arrange your miniatures as nicely as you can, having regard to colours and sizes of blooms of different varieties, and overall an appropriately dainty, fresh appearance. Experience comes with practice but beginners can learn a lot from studying the entries from old hands and, like them, before long get great pleasure from attempting in this final step at the show to present their roses to perfection.

Clay and Lucia Morgan, two of America's top judges, say that in their judging of multi-stem roses they look for blooms that are uniform in size,

For miniature entries at a show you need to have well shaped blooms (unless you are entering the class for sprays) and they must be attractively arranged. This drawing shows a prizewinner at an American Rose Society Show.

shape and stem. If one stem is short don't put it down deep in the vase. A wedge of florist's green tissue paper can be used to hold the stems in place (and this is not cheating) but the wedge should not show above the vase top. Damaged petals and foliage can be trimmed with small, sharp nail scissors. When exhibiting one bloom per stem make sure that there are no side buds. Take out any extra growth. For balance and proportion in this case two or more sets of five-leaflet leaves are desirable. The Morgans' final advice is: if you have a question ask somebody who has exhibited. It helps.

Other important things to look for are:
●The perfect hybrid tea type bloom will be half to three-quarters open; polyanthas and similar rosette shapes which naturally open fully should have stamens of fresh colour, not dark and ageing.
●The blooms and stem should be in proportion — avoid a thick stem and a small bloom or a tiny stem and a big bloom.
●If you are entering a spray instead of a single bloom the only difference is that the buds should be left on the stems. They should be fairly open and showing colour; if you can have them all fresh and at the same stage then you are likely to have a winner.
●Crooked stems are likely to lose points in some cases.

If I had to give words of warning about shows they would be: arrive early, know your schedule and don't be rushed. I know some people who wouldn't think it was a show unless they were running about all over the place, but leading exhibitors rarely do.

When you have your entry ready, put it in its place. There is often a lot of gamesmanship about in shows and I remember the showman who left his best vase of blooms hidden away until the last moment so that other exhibitors would be lulled into a false sense of security. Then he forgot where he had put them!

Something must be said about the different attitudes to the miniature classes — in both their scheduling and their judging. The best format, in my opinion, is that introduced in New Zealand in 1983, where the New Zealand Rose Society sought advice from the top people involved in the showing of miniatures. Now the United States has followed the same line. On 1 January 1985 the US judging rules changed to allow miniatures to be judged in the same way as hybrid teas, with miniature sprays judged as floribundas. There are special classes for single (five-petalled) blooms and open blooms. This is also the New Zealand method. So the classic form of the rose now comes through in the miniatures too with the floribunda style also being acknowledged. In many countries all the roses are grouped together and judged *en masse*, leading to decisions that often surprise the public and leave them wondering how the show was judged. Awkward though it may seem to the untrained eye the actual judging of the varieties against each other does not — or should not — present problems where the judges are thoroughly familiar with the varieties and can assess first-class and not-so-good specimens of each. 'This mixture of varieties,' says Frank Bowen, 'is more difficult but once a judge know his miniatures he can more often than not reach a fair decision.'

The primary aim behind the mixing of the varieties was to make sure that a representative selection would be on view, not only to boost the increasing interest in miniatures but also to help exhibitors and potential judges to get to know them. Segregating the varieties was not possible in the 1970s in Britain because the range available commercially was so much smaller than in the USA or Australia and the number of hybrid tea types in particular was smaller still. Most shows would have ended up with row after row of Starina in the hybrid tea class and nothing else. The policy did achieve its aim by widening the scope of the miniatures enormously, and as more and more of the hybrid tea types become available so the schedules will have to change. But many rose societies are waiting to see the outcome of the New Zealand and the US legislation. Certainly the Royal National Rose Society in Britain is monitoring it carefully as this is the format that Mr Bowen suggested some years ago the Society should eventually aim at.

Judging a rose, whether by qualified judge or by a show visitor, is, in the end, a matter of personal opinion. However, these days, with more and more judges having qualified through examination, there are few classes that are judged by one person. In the major shows throughout the world I have operated in teams of two, three and five people. The panel of three seems best — it is a hard day's work trying to get five people to agree to the worth of a rose! This means that there should today be a better overall standard of judging.

America takes the showing and judging of miniatures very seriously and the number of blooms at even the smaller shows makes it a tough task for any number of judges. While schedules do vary from place to place the most popular way of setting up a show there is in alphabetical order — in other words there will be classes for everything from Ada Perry right through to Zinger. The winners of these classes are then judged against each other for the overall title of miniature Queen of the Show. In the majority of cases all these will be one bloom to a stem although there are classes for sprays and collections too. The most important piece of advice here is to read the schedules thoroughly. The best story I know about someone misreading the schedule (and trying some gamesmanship) is of a famous competitor who heard that so-and-so was to judge a particular class (this was a one-judge affair) and immediately rushed to change his main entry because he believed that the judge in question had a decided preference for one variety. The exhibitor had a vase of red roses ready and hurriedly put them in the class. They looked winners all over, but not in that class. It was for roses other than red! The roses weren't the only red exhibits at the show that afternoon.

There is no doubt that showing is a great hobby and the marvellous thing about miniatures is that you don't need dozens of plants to compete. A few well-chosen varieties will give you all the roses, and excitement, you want. Select them first of all for the form of the rose; classical high-pointed blooms always draw attention and if you can get these on good-growing bushes that are vigorous and produce flowers in abundance you will have winners. My choice would include Starina, Party Girl, Peaches 'n' Cream, Rise 'n' Shine, Red Beauty, Rose Window, Beauty Secret, Starglo and Magic Car-rousel, which are all fairly freely available the world over.

And what varieties would the world's top exhibitors select? In his book *Growing and Showing Roses*, British champion Don Charlton named his selection as Starina, Sheri Anne, Fire Princess, Red Ace (the British version), Darling Flame, Rise 'n' Shine, Judy Fischer, Stacey Sue, Eleanor and Snowdrop. In the United States, the Federation of International Rose Exhibitors named Luis T. Desamero of California as their Exhibitor of the Year for both 1983 and 1984 — and he won the title showing only miniature roses. This was an amazing feat when you consider he was up against top exhibitors who could gain many points with hybrid teas, climbers, floribundas, grandifloras and old garden roses! A quick look at his winning varieties shows that he blends the old very well with the new. Frequently he uses the older varieties like Starina, Beauty Secret, Rise 'n' Shine and Over the Rainbow as well as new varieties such as Party Girl, Jean Kenneally, Holy Toledo, Cupcake, Center Gold, Rainbow's End, Minnie Pearl, Snow Bride, Pacesetter and Red Beauty. And that's as good a guide as you will get anywhere of the top exhibition miniatures.

Don't try too much at your first show by entering a large number of classes. Next year you will know more about it and everything will be so much easier. Finally, remember to keep it fun.

12

ARRANGEMENTS

When in the depths of winter I pick a miniature bloom and wear it in my buttonhole it takes people a long time to realise that the little flower is real. Not only is it out of season but it is so small and perfectly formed. And when miniatures are used for a lady's corsage or for decoration in the house they cause much the same astonishment.

Large dinner-table decorations can get a lot of attention from arrangers only to make the guests bob and duck from one side to another to catch a glimpse of the diner opposite. But a small collection of miniatures suitably arranged along the table can only enhance the occasion. It is not unusual to see the small bouquets being passed from one end of the table to the other as guests appraise the different types of blooms used.

In fact, there is nowhere that you cannot get great benefit from a small number of these tiny blooms. Ten pots, well arranged, will give you a near-endless supply of small flowers that will always be a talking point.

If you have miniature roses indoors make sure that you do have proper miniature containers. It is amazing where you can find these — my own collection ranges from all across the world.

For a while looking in antique shops was my favourite relaxation away from writing and roses. And this is the simple way to pick up small arrangement items. Most people go for larger vases and so often pass by the most suitable containers for miniature roses. For the simple down-to-earth collection look around for the miniature liqueur bottles that come in all shapes and you will get longer pleasure from the container itself than from its original contents. In the same category there used to be small shot glasses; in the Californian gold-country town of Auburn I found two of these with beautiful silver holders engraved with roses. They cost me five dollars.

Tell your friends about your search and it is amazing just how many containers you can gather in a very short time: perfume vials, salt and pepper holders and small mustard pots, shells and candlestick holders. Often cosmetic bottles carry the most unusual stoppers which make perfect miniature vases. Small china animals with cavities, thimbles slightly larger than normal, a doll's tea-pot — the list is limited only by the number of shops you can visit. The items don't have to be in perfect condition; you can quite easily cover up cracks and breaks with a little ingenuity when making the arrangement. Don't make the mistake

Dainty baskets make ideal holders for miniature-rose arrangements. Line the inside with
heavy-duty polythene to make it watertight,
then place in the basket a piece of oasis (or similar material) which can be held in place by green
masking tape.

of allowing the container to drown the
roses. You have to plan both together.
And don't clutter the whole effect with
accessories. Think out your arrangement first; then find your container
and fix it.

But even a shortage of containers
should not in any way stop you using
miniature blooms to their best advantage. At dinner parties one or two
small blooms placed in a piece of oasis
foam wrapped in silver foil make
an inventive posy for the table.
Remember that the holder will only
have to provide sustenance for the
blooms for a few hours, and when the
guests are going they are always
delighted to take their small individual
bouquets with them. Driftwood is
probably one of the most popular
accessories for flower arrangers.
Unfortunately you will seldom find
any that is small enough for miniatures

but those who live near heather land or
grow heathers will know that this can
be the perfect foil, especially if the
foliage has been burnt off. The bare
wood stems will make the same sort of
shapes that you would find in driftwood. I know one lady who found a
wealth of material on a hillside where
the gorse and heather had been burnt in
a summer fire. Look around you; there
are suitable accessories everywhere,
just make sure they are not too big.

These, however, are all fairly basic
ways to use miniatures. In a much
wider scale the miniature has taken a
very special place with floral artists
who really show how they can be used
to the best advantage. Unless you can
find a book on miniature arrangements
look at the more popular general
arrangement books and scale your
work down from there.

The best way to start is with
arrangements that feature two or three
flowers. Some years ago one of my
daughters entered a class in a show that
asked for subjects illustrating book
titles. She chose *The Three Beauties* by
H. E. Bates as her subject; simple,
effective and a winner. Just remember

that the arrangement should finally be one and a half times the height or width of the container, whichever is greater.

Miniatures on their own can be effective but there are a number of plants which can provide foliage to enhance them. I spend a lot of time searching for suitable material but one can always resort to cutting down larger foliage which can be used as long as the stems are not too heavy. Tiny leaf material is what you need; this is often found on house plants so if you see one with suitable foliage, buy it. I always have a fern or two that can be used for this — the wispy growth provides a perfect background for the little blooms. You will need stiffish growth (which doesn't mean big) because mature growth will stand in any arrangement for a much longer time than new, tender material.

The advice given in Chapter 12 about cutting blooms for a show applies here. Cut them, give them a good long drink, groom them and don't go picking them out and putting them back into the holder; make up your mind how the arrangement is going to go and stick to that as closely as possible. The less you handle the

Cheers is its name and this little rose certainly has a cheery look about it. Use three of its bright-orange and cream blooms in a little vase and you have the perfect combination.

Holders for miniatures can be found everywhere – these are tiny replicas of larger holders. The middle one needs some masking tape to hold the oasis in place. In the others, the blooms will stand on their own or can be held in place by discreetly placed paper towels below the rim of the vase. I have found that China, Italy and Spain are the places to find this type of very small holder.

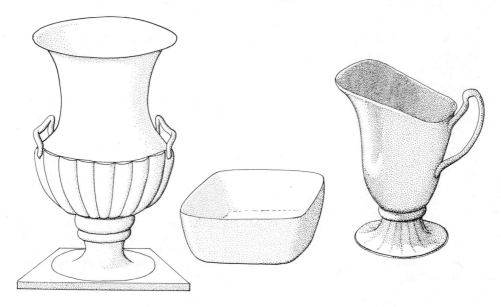

blooms the better they will be and the longer they will last.

Make sure that the material you are using to work your arrangement into has been soaked very well in tepid water with the addition of some flower life additive. This can be bought commercially but a spoonful of sugar in the water is a good substitute. You can also use a bubbly soft drink (I even knew a man once who used watered-down whisky in an effort to preserve his blooms, which didn't work because someone went around behind him drinking the whisky). Whatever you use make sure that the container has been soaked or contains adequate water.

What it is all about in the end is enjoyment of your roses, but do use the blooms as they become ready — the more you cut the more will come.

In the summer when the miniatures are at their very best try dried arrangements. These are so much easier to make nowadays with the arrival of microwave ovens and they take a few minutes from start to finish instead of a week or longer. The microwave provides a very quick drying method for the blooms — about one minute plus some time for them to cool down. The colour is retained remarkably well. Of course, being miniatures you can do so many together in a much smaller area.

Cut the flowers just below the head; you don't need any length of stem as you will be using florist's wire. You will also need silica gel in which to dry them. This can be bought in most florists' shops. Depending on the state of the roses when cut, you can decide whether some of them need opening up. For this I use the end of a very small paint-brush or even a not-too-sharp toothpick. Gently push out the petals so that when they are put in a heat-resistant container there is room for the silica gel to fall in between the petals.

Lay the blooms on a bed of silica gel and pour the remainder of the gel over them. Go very gently because you don't want to damage the petals, and make sure that the gel covers the whole area — don't leave any petals exposed.

Put the container, uncovered, in a microwave oven with a cup of water to provide some humidity (remember that you will need a special cup in the microwave). In just over a minute the job will be completed. Don't leave the flowers too long or they will be too dried. Take them out and leave them to stand until the container is cool, then begin to work on them immediately. Leaving them in the gel will only cause them to dry out further and fall into pieces. As you take the blooms from the container, gently shake away the gel. Run a florist's wire right through each bloom and leave the rose to stand until it is completely dry. The blooms will be quite soft and therefore easy to pierce with the wires. If you need to tape the wire you can easily get florist's tape and wrap it around the bloom from the neck down.

Yellow-and-white and the light-pink miniatures do particularly well. Reds tend to darken very much but they are still useful for inclusion in an arrangement. Roses of blended colours such as Dreamglo, Magic Carrousel and Colibri '79 can be very effective as

When Sam McGredy introduced the 'hand-painted' roses, he gave the world some very different varieties. One of the best of his low growers is Regensberg, named for a Swiss village (the home of flower painter Lotte Gundhart). It grows 12-14in (30-35cm) high, and is covered with delightfully coloured blooms. (*Sam McGredy*)

A corner of the author's garden, with a collection of miniatures in pots of various sizes. All of these were grown from cuttings and were less than one year old when the picture was taken. (*McCann*)

the red edges of their petals darken and the light parts hold their colour.

You will find that they provide beauty right through a whole year and once you have done one lot there will be no stopping you because the dried arrangements and bouquets make lovely presents. Even one bloom is the perfect finish for a beautifully wrapped gift and adds a personal touch to it.

Pot-pourri too is very effective with the petals of little roses and, again, with a microwave the job takes only minutes, though you will need to stir them occasionally to make sure they dry out thoroughly. It is what you add to the dried petals that gives the final product. To about a litre (quart) of rose petals my concoction is a teaspoon of nutmeg, a tablespoon each of powdered cloves, allspice and powdered orris root, and about 2 tablespoons of cinnamon. Build up alternate layers of petals and spices and leave to stand for about a week. Then shake and distribute into whatever holders you choose. A dried bloom added to the pot-pourri makes it look very pretty especially when seen in a glass jar. This way you make sure that your memory of summer is carried through the gloomiest days of winter.

This bee's-eye view gives a good indication of the size of the little flowers of Pixie Rose, an introduction by the Spanish breeder, Pedro Dot. Although losing some of its popularity in the face of the great range of new introductions, this 40 petalled rose is still well worth growing. (*Gregorys*)

13

A ROSE BY ANY OTHER NAME

Miniature roses do have pretty names — there's Rise 'n' Shine, Penny Candy, Razzmataz, Heartland, Baby Darling, Lavender Lace, Little Flirt, Kiss 'n' Tell, Yellow Doll and New Penny, just to mention a few.

But don't be tempted to 'judge the book by its cover'. A name on a rose is the result of a lot of deliberation. Frequently, a new variety arrives on the market with a great name and a great reputation in the breeder's fields but as soon as it becomes public it seems to lose all interest in life. What you find then is that the name sells the rose as opposed to the rose selling the name, and that can be disaster.

That's not to say that the roses named above are not worth growing, and probably you would be drawn by all of them. You won't find Kiss 'n' Tell on the market, however — it happens to be one of mine and is not yet registered. I did not register it initially because the rose that bore the name for three years in the greenhouse turned out to be worthless. I now have a new miniature with this name and I hope that in a year or so it will be good enough to make its public début.

Give a rose a bad name, though, and it takes a lot more effort to get it through to the public. The name that a breeder gives to a rose is not always the

one that sticks with it everywhere. For instance, Irish rose breeder Pat Dickson decided to call a rose Peek-a-Boo, a pretty name for a very pretty copper-coloured miniature (although some catalogues 'officially' list it as a patio dwarf). It's the sort of rose that would grace any garden and is perfect for potting or container growing, needing very little attention other than watering and feeding. It attracted a lot of attention in 1983 and American rose specialists Jackson and Perkins decided to include it in their lists. But they didn't like the name, so when they launched it in America they called it Brass Ring. It may sound a great name in the States but in Northern Ireland it has different connotations altogether. In America if you happen to grab the brass ring as you ride the carousel you are entitled to a free ride next time around. But in Ireland a brass ring suggests a man who wasn't rich enough to buy a gold wedding ring and had to settle for a brass one instead. You can see then why Pat Dickson was not overjoyed when he heard the name picked by J and P.

Now and again a breeder will suddenly think of a very suitable name for a little rose only to find that it is registered for an international product, and that causes problems. American breeder Harmon Saville had an idea for a name but when he made a move to register it the firm who had already used it came down with a ban. Most firms, though, feel that to have a rose variety named after their product can only be good for publicity.

I often wonder how the famous Olympic skating star Dorothy Hamill felt after her agent turned down the opportunity to have her name on a rose. The agent refused, saying that Miss Hamill was not endorsing any products at that time. The variety turned out to be the top-ranking Rise 'n' Shine.

Personalities have not entered the naming of the miniatures as much as they have with the bigger varieties. But English television stars Angela Rippon and Anna Ford have had small roses named for them. Clarissa, a lovely little patio rose (it is registered as a floribunda but for me is definitely a patio rose, a contender of the highest order), is named for Mrs James Mason, while country-and-western star Minnie Pearl had a perfect little pink rose named in her honour in Nashville itself. A famous personality in the American rose world, Jan Shrivers, almost had a rose named for her but she decided instead that it would be better off with a name that everyone could associate with; and so the rose became Party Girl, because Jan is something of a party girl herself.

Californian Ralph Moore has launched more miniatures than anyone else and among the great names he has picked for his roses are a number for personalities. He is probably the only breeder ever to name a rose for a husband and wife. Mary Marshall is a great worker for the rose in the United States and is on national committees of various sorts. On a visit one day to the Moore nurseries she enthused so much about a little apricot mini that Ralph

One of the great attractions of miniatures is the length of time the blooms keep, either in a vase or on the bush. Heartland holds good form and a bright coral colour for a long time.

Moore named it for her. It went on to become one of the top ten roses in the US but didn't make it in Europe where it fell prey to mildew all too easily. Then Ralph Moore decided that Don Marshall, also a great rose enthusiast and exhibitor, deserved a variety too and he gave him a dark red that should do very well. As if that wasn't enough for one family he also named a rose for the Marshall granddaughter — Pink Mandy.

There are also some roses named for commercial enterprises. Sam Mc-Gredy matched his hybrid tea Benson and Hedges Gold with a small rose called Benson and Hedges Special. There is no doubt that the company was pleased enough to sponsor the variety and I'm sure the growers associated with McGredy throughout the world were happy enough to sell roses on the strength of the publicity worked up by the cigarette manufacturer's PR people. The famous French breeders, Meillands, also moved into the commercial tie-up with a number of bigger roses and eventually picked up sponsorship for the light pink miniature Air France from the national airline. Again both sides gained from the publicity. (It should be said that this particular rose isn't a good garden variety; it is much happier in a greenhouse or conservatory.)

Generally speaking, rose breeders have not moved into sponsorship with miniatures with anything like the fervour that some have put into the bigger varieties. They prefer to search for appealing names and while this is quite acceptable there is no doubt that as time goes on so the need for commercial back-up will become greater. The finances from sponsorship will go a long way towards helping to breed more miniatures and hopefully better ones through experimental crossings that are often very expensive. How expensive? Well, a few years ago Jack Harkness of Hitchin in Hertfordshire and the late Alex Cocker of Aberdeen together managed to get a breakthrough with the only red-eyed rose in the world, *Rosa hulthemosa*, a variety that grows mainly in the wild. It looked all over the best chance breeders had had for a long time to break into a new strain of roses but to buy a set would have cost £500. As it turned out the roses proved mulish and only a few have been able to move beyond those original specimens. It should be said, however, that the price of £500 was little against the money, time and enthusiasm put into the scheme initially by Cocker and Harkness.

So commerce is necessary for breeders to succeed but for all that, within the whole business of raising miniatures, amateurs have had notable successes. And when an amateur raises a variety that looks as though it has a chance he looks around for either a family name or a pretty one. For instance, we have Ginny (for a wife), Pacesetter, Cupcake, Peaches 'n' Cream and many others.

But the laws of demand mean that today many old roses are no longer commercially grown and their names have been passed on to other varieties. If you are looking up old records you may well find that a rose you thought was a miniature is in that older book something very different. A lot of good names have gone into the registration of miniatures. There are very few nursery rhyme characters left: Bo Peep, Tom Thumb, Red Riding Hood, Jack Horner and even Humpty Dumpty adorn little roses. Some breeders now use a symbol or a name almost exclusively. Ernest Williams in Texas is known for his roses that are suffixed 'glo': as in Dreamglo, Gloriglo, Loveglo. Sam McGredy is now picking Maori names such as Kaikoura; Meillands have a large collection that begin with Mei. There were about twenty-five roses called Little-something at the last count and about fifteen Baby-whatevers. The shortest name is probably Si.

And what about Angel Dust? It sounds pretty but in fact is a name for a deadly drug. Hybridiser Dee Bennett said that she had no idea what it really meant: 'I never would have put such a curse on one of my babies. By the time I was informed that the term 'angel dust' referred to a deadly narcotic it was too late . . . the rose had been registered. I still do not understand why someone at the American Rose Society did not stop the registration of this lovely rose or at least contact me before authorising such a horrible mistake.

Perhaps they were as naïve as I was . . .' But for all its troubles Angel Dust still holds a place in many catalogues, probably because in this case the rose was able to live down its unfortunate name.

The rose world will never run out of names — after all horse-racing sheets alone manage to provide a whole collection of names on any given day. Street Angel, Pretty Face, Rainbow Quest, Tropical Mist, Pride 'n' Joy, Dragon Fire and Elegant Air were all picked from one list of runners! But that won't guarantee that either the horse or the rose will be a winner!

14

HOW THEY RATE THEM

Each year American Rose Society members receive a tabulation called 'Proof of the Pudding'. It has nothing to do with recipes for rose dishes but is a listing and rating for most of the roses in commerce.

Miniatures figure largely in this report and some of the newer varieties are moving in on the longtime leader, the French-bred Starina. Any day now it is likely that a fairly recent variety like Rise 'n' Shine, Rainbow's End, Cupcake or Party Girl will become the number one. At present Starina merits 9.4 (out of 10) followed by Beauty Secret with 9.3.

Proof of the Pudding is something that Americans watch very carefully for indications of a variety heading fast up the list, or for suggestions that another may be dropping out of favour. The ratings are tabulated from reports received from the country's eighteen regional rose societies. During the year each member receives a form to fill in, giving a report on the varieties they have grown, taking into account garden display rating, number of years grown, vigour, disease-resistance, bloom production and bloom repeat, hardiness, fragrance, and what is liked and what is disliked about the variety. The most telling question of all is 'will you keep it?' Points earned as

a result of the answers go to make the final POP rating.

The final figure achieved by each variety is published in a small booklet that is a perfect addition to the usual data available about the different roses. While the booklet gives only the tabulation figures, some of the reports and comments are published each year in the *Rose Annual*, and they can be quite merciless.

For instance, a dark red miniature called Fireball was said in 1982 to be insufficiently reported but, said co-ordinator Louis C. Gross, what was reported included a 'YUK' from New York and the rest was alarming! Foxy Lady, a pink blend, achieved 7.0 for garden display and 7.5 for exhibition, but more was expected. 'Maybe the name is a clue to the performance,' wrote the co-ordinator, 'the plant can be a treasure in one garden and a disappointment next door. Generally it needs more petals to the bloom, more blooms to the plant and it usually opens too rapidly.' Other miniatures in the 1982 Proof of the Pudding were dismissed for 'terminal lethargy', and for looking like a 'multicoloured Christmas tree all summer', and one unfortunate received the comment: 'Even collectors may find it difficult to overlook the frequent lack of vigour, the insufficiency of bloom and the depressed centers.'

And the same sort of straight talking is found in all other years of the POP review. With that sort of honesty the most famous rose breeder in the world won't get away with it if he puts out a dud.

Of course, there is the positive side to all this — when a variety is good it gets high marks and the comments will tell you why gardeners consider it so good.

Take the pink blend Baby Katie for instance. In one year it doubled the number of its admirers and also improved its ratings, and the co-ordinator wrote: 'I believe the ratings will rise when the exhibition potential of this . . . is perceived.' The other good points of Baby Katie included 'always in bloom', 'high marks from everyone' and 'delicacy is part of its charm.' So when the points were tabulated Baby Katie had 8.0 for garden use and 8.5 for exhibition, and the appreciation of this one throughout the world has not diminished.

The arrival of the mid-pink Cupcake brought this comment from the 1983 co-ordinator, Mrs Muriel Humenick: 'I knew if we could just hang in there long enough with the minis we would come up with a winner.' One reporter said that it was 'almost perfect — the only thing missing is fragrance'. Cupcake is now taking so many top prizes in American shows that there can be little doubt that it will be among the tops for some time to come. Its colour, variously described as 'yummy', 'frosty' and 'delicious' says something else about it. Its ratings in 1983, its first year in the POP, were 8.0 for garden use and 8.1 for exhibition, a stunning introduction that had Mrs Humenick commenting: 'Move over Starina.'

Apart from the Proof of the Pudding ratings there is another tabulation in the United States that is keenly awaited by miniature lovers. This comes from the Golden Triangle Rose Society of south-west Texas and is a table of all the top prizewinning roses in the US, made up from reports received by the American Rose Society from every show organised throughout the country. Scoring is on a basis of 6 points for the best rose, 5 for the second and 4 for the third. In the returns for the 1983 season the Golden Triangle had 130 miniatures named as top medal certificate winners.

The listing was headed by Party Girl which had almost 160 points more in shows than the ubiquitous Starina, which was in second place. Although Party Girl currently merits only 8.5 for exhibition in the POP ratings, it is moving very fast towards the top rating. It is a versatile rose producing one bloom of perfect proportions per stem or a whole spray of little wonders.

After this on the Golden Triangle list came twenty-three varieties as shown (where possible the POP rating for exhibition that was right at the time has been included although many of them may have improved on these ratings since then):

Golden Triangle List

1 Party Girl (8.5)
2 Starina (9.4)
3 Dreamglo (8.0)
4 Rise 'n' Shine (8.5)
5 Magic Carrousel (8.9)
6 Red Beauty (recent 7.9)
7 Minnie Pearl (new)
8 Pacesetter (8.0)
9 Peaches 'n' Cream (8.0)
10 Beauty Secret (9.3)
11 Judy Fischer (8.8)
    Toy Clown (8.9)
12 Mary Marshall (8.7)
13 Puppy Love (8.0)
14 Starglo (8.6)

15	Baby Katie (8.0)	
16	Cupcake (8.0)	
17	Simplex (8.8)	
18	Kathy Robinson (8.8)	
	Over the Rainbow (8.5)	
19	Rose Window (7.5)	
20	Fairlane (8.0)	
	Popcorn (8.1)	
21	Acey Duecy (no rating as yet)	
	Cinderella (8.7)	

In Great Britain the Rose Analysis published by the Royal National Rose Society is the only available tabulation of the top miniatures. While the varieties have shown little change in recent years there is no doubt that the influx of new varieties over the next year or so will cause many changes in this table.

Already at shows throughout Britain some of the American-raised roses like Peaches 'n' Cream, Mary Marshall, Dreamglo and others, although not commercially available, have been making their marks. These blooms were from bushes of the 'plant hunters', those rose lovers who have linked themselves with friends throughout the world and find that after their holidays they have acquired some small piece of a new rose! It may not be entirely legal — there are stringent laws against the importation of plants without health certificates — but it is done. And these growers are not breaking any patent laws as they are just growing the varieties for their own pleasure; if they sold them that would be a different story.

As is probably to be expected, the top miniature variety according to the Royal National Rose Society Analysis published in the *Rose Annual* is Meilland's Starina, some 160 points ahead of the same breeder's Darling Flame (also called Minuetto).

Royal National Rose Society's Analysis

1 Starina
2 Darling Flame (Minuetto)
3 Magic Carrousel
4 Rise 'n' Shine
5 Angela Rippon
6 Baby Masquerade
  Stacey Sue
8 Pour Toi
9 Easter Morning
10 Red Ace (not to be confused with a US variety of the same name)
11 Rosina
12 Fire Princess
13 Judy Fischer

I have no doubts that recent introductions such as Snowdrop, Wee Barbie, Peek-a-Boo (Brass Ring) and Longleat (Wanaka) will enter this list to the exclusion (in my opinion) of Rosina, Easter Morning and possibly Pour Toi. The others all deserve their placings and can be fully recommended for garden and exhibition.

There is real enthusiasm for the miniatures in Canada where gardeners have the selection of the best in the world. The President of the Canadian Rose Society, Mrs Ethel Freeman, finds that they are attracting more and more interest at shows, especially at a national level. Miniature roses have a special place there because they are more winter hardy than many of the hybrid teas or floribundas. Mrs Freeman says that they do need some winter protection but not much; a shovelful of loose earth or hard leaves will do the trick, and the miniatures are always the first to leaf out in the spring.

The only grower in Canada who has mixed hybridising with selling is Keith Laver of Springwood Roses in Mississauga, Ontario. As well as his own five introductions he offers over 120 other varieties. If you want to find out exactly how these flourish under Canadian conditions you turn to the section in their *Rose Annual* called the Clearing House. This is very much on the lines of the American POP with detailed analyses of the top roses. The review of the roses in the 1983 annual looked at over 100 varieties, going all the way from Andrea to Zinger, and included many varieties that I have not seen commented upon anywhere else. It is a mine of information for the miniature-rose enthusiast.

The New Zealand method of analysis is very similar to the British but their annual does contain some pithy comments about new varieties. New Zealanders possibly haven't yet come to terms with the miniatures — male exhibitors still tend to refer to them as 'women's roses'. This is something that will change, and very quickly, especially as rosarians there are able to purchase a far greater range of roses than rosarians in Britain. They also have the advantage of having Sam McGredy on their doorstep and he is producing a whole range of small roses; below are some of the markings for new McGredy varieties that I have not seen anywhere else:

Kaikoura 7.5. Vivid orange-red and rather large.

Ko's Yellow 7.9. Despite good reports from other places this one disappointed the New Zealander commentator, Don Sheppard.

Moana 7.0. A low mark despite the comments that it makes an ideal garden subject.

Otago 7.0. Low again, though it is described as a welcome addition to the miniature range.

Takapuna 7.4. This little peach-pink is said to be always in bloom.

Wanaka 7.0. A low rating, although when this one arrived at a recent sale of plants in the United States it was quickly being snapped up because of its vivid flame-red bloom and neat bush.

This is one of those unfortunate roses that is saddled with a number of names — in Britain it is Longleat and in Canada it is Young Cole.

Another New Zealand variety that I haven't seen anywhere else is Cecile Lens, a pale pink that has achieved an 8.3 rating. It comes from the Belgian raiser Louis Lens and is a variety that deserves wider publicity. But for all its beauty and high marks Cecile Lens has not achieved a place in the top ten of the New Zealand roses.

In the New Zealand analysis of miniatures over fifty-nine varieties were reported and the following got the top marks:

1 Starina
2 Magic Carrousel
3 Mary Marshall
4 Beauty Secret
5 Kaikoura
6 Rise 'n' Shine
7 Over the Rainbow
8 Starglo
9 Sunmaid
10 Wanaka

Dawn and Barry Eagle, who run Christchurch's Southern Cross Nursery, list about seventy-two varieties — by far the biggest number of miniatures on sale in the country. They include one of their own breeding, Selwyn Toogood, which is pink and lightly mossed.

Of all the countries where I have seen miniatures growing, New Zealand seems more prepared to let them grow as big as they want to. In some gardens bushes of miniatures were up to 120cm (4ft) high. The growth did not inhibit the production of blooms — the plants were covered with flowers. Maybe we should let miniatures have their heads more often and see how nature wants them to grow!

Australia does not have a national rating system as such but the six regional societies — Victoria, South Australia, New South Wales, Queensland, Western Australia and Tasmania — do produce annual lists of recommended roses for their members. These are published in their *Rose Annual*. Some of the societies produce a list of the top twelve, others are more generous, going as high as twenty-four, and also suggest some new varieties worthy of trial.

An analysis of these figures by Mr J. L. Priestly of the National Rose Society of Australia provided this listing, in alphabetical order, of the top ten: Avandel, Beauty Secret, Dwarf King, Green Ice, Lavender Lace, Magic Carrousel, Mary Marshall, Over the Rainbow, Rosmarin and (as if anyone could miss it) Starina.

Roy Rumsey, a leading grower in Australia, remembers that the first miniature grown on his father's nursery was *Rosa rouletii*. Through the 1960s more varieties arrived and later Roy's wife, Heather, took a great interest in the new varieties from America; soon they had a big listing of miniatures as well as other types of rose.

American breeder Ralph Moore believes that Australia's enthusiasm at the beginning of the boom led to more miniatures being grown there than anywhere else in the world. Today the country still grows a large number of miniatures and the Rumsey rose firm offers over seventy varieties for sale. Surprisingly enough, many of these are being used by the cut-flower trade, a fairly recent development that is also seen in South Africa. One interesting addition to the miniatures boom is that Roy Rumsey grows his standard or tree miniatures on a 30cm (12in) stem as opposed to the normal 40cm (16in) or 45cm (18in) used elsewhere. He believes that the 30cm (12in) stem shows up the little roses while the taller stems detract from the beauty of the blooms.

The listings for the regional rose groups in Australia, as given below, do carry some interesting varieties that are not seen elsewhere, like Wee Beth which is a variety from the amateur breeder Eric Walsh and is, I believe, the only Australian-bred rose in the miniature classes.

The Rose Society of Victoria
(twelve varieties)
Baby Darling, Galaxy, Gold Coin, Green Ice, Jeanne Lajoie (climber), Magic Carrousel, Mary Marshall, Over the Rainbow, Perla de Montserrat, Scarlet Gem, Starina, Zwergkonig (Dwarf King).
Worthy of trial: Baby Bettina and Rise 'n' Shine.

The Rose Society of South Australia Incorporated
(eighteen varieties)
Beauty Secret, Coral Treasure, Cream Gold, Gipsy Jewel, Green Ice, Hula Girl, Kathy, Lavender Jewel, Magic Carrousel, Mary Marshall, Over the Rainbow, Persian Princess, Stacey Sue, Starina, Sundust, Sunmaid, Westmont, Yellow Doll.
Worthy of trial: Double Joy, Red Flush and Strawberry Swirl.

The Rose Society of New South Wales *(twenty-one varieties)*
Avandel, Beauty Secret, Cricket, Golden Angel, Green Ice, Hula Girl, Judy Fischer, Lavender Jewel, Magic Carrousel, Mary Marshall, My Valentine, Over the Rainbow, Petite Folie, Rise 'n' Shine, Rosmarin, Sheri Anne, Starina, Star Trail, Watercolour, Wee Beth, Whipped Cream.
Worthy of trial: Baby Katie, Galaxy, Holy Toledo and Party Girl.

The Queensland Rose Society
(twenty-one varieties)
Baby Darling, Baby Gold Star, Coral Treasure, Cream Gold, Fashion Flame, Fiesta Ruby, Gold Coin, Green Ice, Happy Thought, Kathy, Lavender Lace, Magic Carrousel, My Valentine, Persian Princess, Petite Folie, Rosmarin, Silver Tips, Starina, Sunmaid, White Madonna, Zwergkonig (Dwarf King).
Worthy of trial: Avandel and Meillandia.

The Rose Society of Western Australia *(eighteen varieties)*
Avandel, Firefall, Golden Angel, Happy Thought, Hula Girl, Lavender Jewel, Magic Carrousel, Mary Marshall, Orange Cascade, Over the Rainbow, Rosmarin, Scarlet Gem, Starina, Star Trail, Strawberry Swirl, Sunmaid, The Fairy, Wee Beth.
Worthy of trial: Orange Honey and Puppy Love.

The Rose Society of Tasmania
(twenty-two varieties)
Avandel, Baby Gold Star, Beauty Secret, Carol-Jean, Dresden Doll, Golden Angel, Green Ice, Judy Fischer, June Time, Lavender Jewel, Lavender Lace, Magic Carrousel, Mary Marshall, Over the Rainbow, Para Ti (Pour Toi), Perla de Montserrat, Petite Folie, Rise 'n' Shine, Sheri Anne, Starina, Toy Clown, Zwergkonig (Dwarf King).
Worthy of trial: Coral Treasure, My Valentine, Stacey Sue and Sunny Morning.

South Africa is one of the few countries where Starina does not hold court at the top of the table; pride of place goes here to the de Ruiter-bred Ocarina, better known elsewhere as Angela Rippon. Ludwig Taschner, who apart from being secretary to the World Federation of Rose Societies also heads a large nursery, provided this order of merit: Angela Rippon, Starina, Rise 'n' Shine, Rosmarin, Petite Folie, Galaxy, Amoretta, Baby Masquerade, Magic Carrousel, Scarlet Gem.

This listing is likely to change very quickly with the arrival in the country of many more of the American-bred varieties as well as the widespread offer of the rosamini and minimo selections from de Ruiter. Here also the in-between varieties have been causing a lot of interest and the South Africans have their own name for them, calling the group midinette roses. I like too the name that Mrs Taschner gave to the miniature roses that she is particularly interested in — Sunspot roses. In all there are about eighty different varieties of miniatures on sale in the country.

15

MY TOP THIRTY

Every year more and more new miniature roses arrive on the market in a continuous line of introductions. In 1983 alone there were about seventy new varieties, far more than any other type of rose. Add that to the hundreds that have already been produced since the mid-seventies when miniatures achieved far greater prominence, and also add in the many hundreds available before that, and you will realise that making a selection is almost mind-boggling.

If you look at the normal catalogues of miniatures for sale the prospect of sorting them out so that a recommended thirty or forty can be given is not enticing. One list from Miniature Plant Kingdom in Sabastopol, California contains over 500 varieties of the bush type alone and about 20 of climbing miniatures!

So my criterion for selecting a variety for this special list was simple enough — the rose would have to have proven itself right across the world so that if you grow it in Dallas or Delhi, Dresden or 'Derry, you can be pretty sure that it will give you good results.

The details given below include the hybridiser's name and the date of introduction, the rose's breeding (where possible), a description of form and my own comments. When a number is given following the description, ie Starina . . . 9.4, this refers to the rating given in the 1984 Proof of the Pudding issued by the American Rose Society. While ratings can vary quite considerably with bigger roses from climate to climate the miniatures are pretty standard everywhere. If there is a likely variation I have mentioned this too. Some varieties which I have selected are not, as yet, rated.

I have begun with the rose generally credited with being the starter of the modern miniatures:

R. rouletii Small, double rose-red. Grows to about 30cm (12in) high. A little beauty whose ancestry is uncertain. Could well be *R. chinensis minima* — but then again might not be! Nevertheless a starting point for miniatures and still worth growing. 8.0.

Angela Rippon (also known as Ocaru and Ocarina) Salmon-pink. de Ruiter, 1976. Rosy Jewel x Zorina. A vigorous, bushy grower. Double blooms in good clusters. Regarded in many parts of the world as one of the very best, especially in South Africa where it is number one. Deserves at least a rating of 8.0.

Baby Darling Salmon-orange. R. S. Moore, 1964. Little Darling x Magic Wand. Dwarf, bushy 20.3–30.5cm (8–

12in). Double flowers. When anyone tells you that miniatures get mildew here is just one that will disprove it. This little plant grows well with very pretty blooms. 8.5.

Baby Katie Pink blend. H. Saville, 1978. Sheri Anne x Watercolour. Bushy, compact and vigorous, with very prolific blooms. A lovely high-centred bloom even though it has only 12 petals; the little flower holds and holds. 8.0.

Beauty Secret Cardinal red. R. S. Moore, 1965. Little Darling x Magic Wand. Vigorous and bushy. Flower double, high-centred and fragrant. Here is a miniature to measure most others against. The bright medium-red bloom on an upright plant makes it a top show winner. A sister seedling to Baby Darling. 9.3.

Cinderella Satin-white tinged with shell-pink. J. de Vink, 1953. Cecile Brunner x Tom Thumb. A perfectly balanced, very bushy plant; thornless. Small double blooms (40–60 petals); fragrant. Don't take anyone's word that you should keep this one underfed so that it remains small. Looks just as wonderful when in the best of health and full of disease-resistant and lovely little blooms that begin a shell-pink and finish white. 8.7.

Cupcake Pink. M. Spies, 1981. Gene Boerner x (Gay Princess x Yellow Jewel). Compact, bushy and thornless. Vigorous growth with good foliage. Profuse bloom, high-centred, double long-lasting flowers (50–65 petals) in that lovely pink-icing colour and beautifully shaped. 8.0.

Darling Flame (also known as Minuetto) Bright orange. Meilland, 1971. (Rimosa x Rosina) x Zambra. Probably Europe's most popular miniature variety. An eye-catcher with deep vermilion-orange blooms and gold reverse, it grows on a well-shaped and vigorous, free flowering bush.

Also a great provider of modern miniatures and floribunda roses, especially for Harkness Roses who have used the pollen very effectively. 7.2.

Earthquake Red and yellow stripes. R. S. Moore, 1983. Golden Angel x (Dortmund x seedling). Free flowering and bushy plant. No two flowers alike. The first of the red and yellow striped miniatures (I'm sure there will be more). Named soon after an earthquake at Coalinga in central California near Visalia where the famous Moore nurseries are based. Potentially a very good variety.

Easter Morning Ivory-white. R. S. Moore, 1960. Golden Glow x Zee. Glossy and leathery foliage. About 60 petals. It is highly disease resistant and has been well tested over the years. If it has a fault it is that it may not produce the abundance of blooms that other varieties do, but for all that it is worthy of a place in this list. 7.8.

Eleanor Pink. R. S. Moore, 1960. (R. wichuraiana x Floradora) x (seedling x Zee). Upright, bushy, free flowering. Tiny coral-pink blooms that seem to be forever attractive. About 20 petals that last well and darken with age. This plant is quite happy in all weathers. 7.1.

Holy Toledo Apricot blend. J. Christensen, 1978. Gingersnap x Magic Carrousel. Prolific urn-shaped bloom with 25–30 petals. Vigorous growth. An eye-catching plant that gets its place because of shape, colour and good disease resistance. 8.5.

Hula Girl Orange. Ernest D. Williams, 1976. Miss Hillcrest x Mabel Dot. Long-pointed bud, 45 petals. Medium fragrance. Glossy foliage. A very good bushy-growing variety that smiles at the weather no matter what it is. 7.7

Judy Fischer Deep pink. R. S. Moore, 1968. Little Darling x Magic Wand (a much used cross in early work by Ralph Moore). Vigorous, bushy with dark bronze foliage. The shapely blooms, profuse and non-fading, make this variety one of the best for edging or a small short hedge. Grows to about 25–30cm (10–12in) high. 8.8.

Kaikoura Red blend. S. McGredy, 1978. Anytime x Matangi. Bushy, vigorous, dark green foliage, 27 petals. One of several McGredy-introduced miniatures named for New Zealand locations: the others are Otago, Wanaka, Waitemeta and Moana.

Ko's Yellow Yellow. S. McGredy, 1977. (New Penny x Banbridge) x (Border Flame x Manx Queen). Bushy, very full growth, glossy foliage. A hybrid tea shape with about 40 petals. Very interesting for the variation in breeding which is completely different from the American hybridising lines.

Lavender Lace Lavender. R. S. Moore, 1968. Ellen Poulsen x Debbie. Bushy and dwarf. Small, double, high-centred bloom. Fragrant; delightful colour with lots of petals (over 50). My problem with this vigorous plant is that I can't throw away a cutting and I finish each year with far more plants than I can possibly handle. For many this one has been replaced by Lavender Jewel, also from Ralph Moore, but I still like the original best. 7.8.

Longleat (also known as Wanaka and Young Cole) Red. S. McGredy, 1978. Anytime x Trumpeter. A bright little flame-red that catches the eye at a distance. In the style of many of the early McGredy miniatures in that it can grow a little too big for many people, but I know that in New Zealand they wouldn't agree — and in Britain it hasn't done too badly either.

Magic Carrousel Red and white. R. S. Moore, 1972. Little Darling x Westmont. Strong stems, continuous bloom. Foliage small. Grows to about 45cm (18in) high. Hardy and reliable is a good phrase to use for this very pretty white-and-red-tipped variety. Tends to grow a bit leggy and must be controlled by sensible pruning that doesn't allow it to lose its way. 8.9.

Mary Marshall Orange blend. R. S. Moore, 1970. Little Darling x Fairy Princess. Vigorous, dwarf, bushy. Long-pointed bud, cupped bloom. Named for one of America's top rose growers and administrators. A super little rose even though outside America it does seem to need a special watch for mildew — but with today's spray programme there should be no trouble taking care of that. 8.7.

Over the Rainbow Red and yellow. R. S. Moore, 1972. Little Darling x Westmont (same as Magic Carrousel). Very good form if slightly large blooms. Upright. Healthy. This very bright little rose has done its work well over the years for both gardeners and exhibitors. It has been a great starter for many other miniatures produced by Ernest Williams of the United States.

Pacesetter White. E. Schwartz, 1979. Ma Perkins x Magic Carrousel. Bushy, vigorous and compact. Long-pointed bud that opens high-centred, 43–48 petals. Many people consider that this one gets a little too big in the flower, but not for me — the form makes it a great favourite. Hybridised by one of the great amateurs of miniature breeding, the late Ernie Schwartz. 8.0.

Party Girl Apricot blend. H. Saville, 1979. Rise 'n' Shine x Sheri Anne. Compact and bushy growth. Bud long and pointed. High-centred bloom, 20–25 petals. When you are looking for an exhibition-type miniature this is one that must be considered. Blooms come one to a stem on a nice long presentation. The apricot yellow is sometimes flushed with pink.

Well deserved its Award of Excellence from the American Rose Society in 1981. 7.5.

Peaches 'n' Cream Pink Blend. E. Woolcock, 1976. Little Darling x Magic Wand. Vigorous growth. High-centred bloom (50–55 petals), creamy when opened. Exhibition form, long lasting. A variety that really loves the sun and dislikes the rain. If you have an intemperate climate then keep it under glass. It makes a super little plant for a greenhouse or conservatory. If you ever dream of winning the top prize at a show this is surely the one that will do it for you with its full, well-rounded blooms. 8.0.

Peek-a-Boo (also known as Brass Ring) Orange blend. P. Dickson, 1981. (Bangor x Korbell) x Nozomi. Upright, arching growth. Pointed bud, opening flat, 25–30 petals. The start, it is claimed, of a long line of great miniatures from Northern Ireland's Pat Dickson, famed before this for big hybrid teas such as Red Devil and Grandpa Dickson (also known as Irish Gold). This one has a lovely decoratively shaped bloom, tall and elegant. It was sold as both a miniature and a floribunda but is accepted well within the miniature rating (it is also exhibited as one) and certainly acts like one for me.

Popcorn White. Dr Dennison Morey, 1975. Katherine Zimet x Diamond Jewel. A vigorous and compact little bush with upright growth. Honey fragrance. Profuse blooming all summer long, very dense foliage. If you have seen popcorn in a sweet shop you've seen the rose. I don't know another more truly named. This is a mass of tiny, creamy-white single blooms with bright yellow stamens. 8.1.

Pour Toi (also known as Wendy, For You and Para Ti) White. P. Dot, 1946. Eduardo Toda x Pompon de Paris. Very bushy, glossy foliage. 15 petals. An old one and a very good one that gets its high marks not just for staying the course through the years but for always producing a beautifully shaped bloom, lots of flowers and a nicely shaped bush. 6.3 (but worth more in Great Britain where it is still very highly regarded).

Rise 'n' Shine Yellow. R. S. Moore, 1977. Little Darling x Yellow Magic. Bushy growth. Long-pointed bud. Abundant bloom, excellent exhibition quality. Rich, deep colour — the yellow by which I measure all yellows. My favourite miniature and one I will always give space to. If you want to breed some miniatures this is the one to consider — it sets seeds easily and the seeds also germinate. Don't be put off by the experts who say that it produces a poorly shaped seedling; it also produces some very well-shaped ones. May need protection from black spot. 8.5.

Rose Window Orange blend. Ernest D. Williams, 1978. Seedling x Over the Rainbow. Spreading, bushy growth. Hybrid tea shaped blooms, 25–30 petals. Here's a great winner at shows. The blooms are really eye-catching, have marvellous form and are hard to beat for excellence although the absolute purist may say that the flowers are a little too big. I think most gardeners will like them. 7.5.

Starina Vermilion-scarlet. Meilland, 1965. (Dany Robin x Fire King) x Perla de Montserrat. Foliage glossy; vigorous bush. Small, double blooms. The standard number one miniature for many years. Everybody's favourite, everywhere in the world. The flowers are produced all summer long and it is vigorous up to a certain stage — some plants fail to live much longer than three to four years, but that won't decrease its very high rating. 9.4.

16

LIKELY TO SUCCEED

Because there have been so many new roses introduced in the miniature range in the past five years many of them have not really had a proper chance to show what they can do in public. On the market at the moment there is a whole wealth of lovely little roses; some are destined for glory, others will probably never be heard of again. The following selection of recently introduced varieties includes those that I think are worth considering and the ones that I feel are most likely to succeed:

Avandel Creamy-yellow and peach. R. S. Moore. Compact bush with good foliage. The delicate blooms are very prolific.

Baby Eclipse Yellow. R. S. Moore. Lovely buds and shape. Don't be deceived by the 'Baby' — it is a very strong grower and much taller than most.

Big John Red. Ernest D. Williams. Starburst x Over the Rainbow. Well shaped with abundant growth and bloom production.

Black Jade Very dark red. Frank Benerdella. Awarded the big 'E'.

Born Free Orange-red. R. S. Moore. Red Pinocchio x Little Chief. A good variety for the garden where it gives plenty of bloom.

Carnival Parade Yellow blend. Ernest D. Williams. Starburst x Over the Rainbow. The same breeding as Big John but different in colour and with more spreading growth.

Center Gold Yellow. H. Saville. Rise 'n' Shine x Kiskadee. A cluster-flowering and also a good single rose. Keeps on growing and blooming.

Centerpiece Medium to dark red. H. Saville. High centred, long lasting blooms on a compact plant.

Chattem Centennial Orange-red. N. F. Jolly. Orange Sensation x Zinger. Bright, colourful and a lovely sight with 35-petal blooms.

Dreamglo Red blend. Ernest D. Williams. Little Darling x Little Chief. Good-growing bush, abundant bloom with a lovely red and silver flower.

Freegold Deep yellow. S. Mc-Gredy. Seaspray x Dorola. Lovely small blooms that are fragrant. Also an off-beat breeding line.

Galaxy Deep red. R. S. Moore. Fairy Moss x Fire Princess. Bushy, vigorous and a good repeater. One I really like.

Center Gold, a very good variety whether you want clusters of bloom, or singles with hybrid-tea perfection of shape. To get one-to-a-stem blooms, you must disbud and concentrate the power of the bush into the blooms. (*H. Saville*)

Ginny Red blend. F. J. Bischoff. Little Darling x Toy Clown. Bushy plant, good repeat bloom of a well-shaped flower in white with red edges.

Helen Boehm Light pink. J. Christiensen. Foxy Lady x Deep Purple. A lovely colour and form. May need extra protection in very cold places.

Hot Shot Orange-red. Dee Bennett. Futura x Orange Honey. A nice breeding break and an exhibition winner all the way.

Jean Kenneally Apricot. Dee Bennett. This is a rose that must have a great future as a show variety, perfect blooms in hybrid tea shape. Named for a well known Californian rosarian and judge — indeed we once judged the miniature classes together at Escandito, California.

Lavender Simplex Lavender. Ernest Williams. Beautiful 5-petalled variety.

Little Jackie Orange-yellow. H. Saville. Shapely hybrid tea type blooms on a hardy plant.

Loving Touch Apricot. Nelson Jolly.

Lynne Gold Medium yellow. R. S. Moore. Tiny, pointed buds on a near-thornless plant. A small one for any garden spot or pot.

Minnie Pearl Light pink. H. Saville. (Little Darling x Tiki) x Party Girl. Superb form. Plant sprawls a little but that does not cause any problem. Colour variable from very light pink to near white at times.

Orange Honey Orange blend. R. S. Moore. Rumba x Over the Rainbow. A distinctive bloom that really gives its colour when out of full sunlight.

Plum Duffy Mauve. Dee Bennett. Magic Carrousel self seedling. This is one of my favourite colours, so no apologies for adding this unusual one to my list. Breeders should note that it was one of those seedlings that come when you are least expecting them.

Pucker Up Orange-red. Dee Bennett. Long-stemmed classic-shaped blooms that don't fade. It is a big plant that will do well in the garden as well as on the exhibition table.

Rainbow's End Lemon-yellow, tipped scarlet. H. Saville. Perfect exhibition-type bloom.

Red Beauty Deep red. Ernest D. Williams. Starburst x Over the Rainbow. Long stems, fine shape. May get a touch of mildew but a real winner in the garden or on the show bench.

Snow Bride White. Betty Jolly. Likely big winner, and good garden rose.

Snowdrop White. de Ruiter. Maybe not the best name for a rose but a highly acclaimed newcomer.

Starstruck Orange, red and yellow blend. Dee Bennett. Vigorous and eyecatching.

Sweet Chariot Lavender. R. S. Moore. Spreading and very fragrant.

Tracey Wickham Orange-red with yellow reverse. Eric Welsh. Avandel x (Avandel x Redgold). Cluster flowering giving well shaped single blooms. Full petalled and fragrant. Highly thought of in Australia, it was hybridised in New South Wales.

Winsome Deep mauve. H. Saville. Will make a great impression, though blooms possibly a little large.

The lovely Ballerina, a shrub rose that grows low enough to make an ideal patio subject. It also makes a fine garden subject, carrying trusses of bloom right through the flowering year. (*Fryers*)

17

THE IN-BETWEEN ROSES

Five years ago the distinctions between roses, such as hybrid teas, floribundas, shrubs, climbers and miniatures were obvious. You could quite easily tell to which classification a rose belonged. But in that short space of time we have reached a point in rose breeding where the distinctions are blurred and it is very hard to tell where miniature roses begin and where they end. All this came about because of the fairly recent success of the miniatures. Suddenly hybridisers saw that there was a market for the little ones and they saw, too, that there were opportunities to experiment with different crossings.

So in breeding houses throughout the world hybridisers began to play about with the pollen of the big roses which, when crossed with the miniatures, frequently gave in-between varieties. Others tried the other way around — miniature pollen on to larger type roses — and they too produced a number of roses that were neither floribundas, hybrid teas or miniatures. The breeders did not know what to call these roses. Some tried the ruse of advertising them as both floribundas and miniatures. It was left to one grower in the United States, Benjamin Williams of Maryland, to step in and label them 'Minifloras'. This was a very good group name but by claiming

it for himself Mr Williams effectively prevented its use by the rest of the world's growers. Another very good name, 'Maxi-Minis' was patented by Gene King, a Louisiana pharmacist and hybridiser. He registered the first two roses under this trade mark in November 1984 — Heartlight and Fantasie.

So the rush began to find another name that would express exactly what these roses are. Cushion roses, sweetheart, minimo, rosamini, macrominia all achieved a place in catalogues somewhere or other but one very good name was passed over — petitflora, suggested in the *American Rose Magazine* by a former president of the San Francisco Rose Society, Rose Gilardi. In South Africa they were calling them midinette roses. However, the name that everyone seemed to want to use was 'patio' rose in the belief that 'if you keep calling them patio roses people will begin to realise that roses do make good patio subjects — otherwise they might never have thought of growing them there'. Of course there had to be opposition to this name, based on the sound commercial principle that more people have gardens than have patios; by suggesting they were patio roses, growers were eliminating their use in gardens. The name patio may last, but not for long. In France, Meillands heavily promoted this type of rose by calling it a Meillandina, offering just about every colour in the range.

Soon, however, the Meillandina roses and the miniflora got together under the banner of Conard-Pyle's Star Roses in the USA, who sold both the Benjamin Williams' roses and the Meilland varieties, and issued some very effective publicity material for them. The recommendation for the culture of these roses was that they should be grown in 8cm (3in) pots but if forcing was considered then the pot size should be increased. They were sold growing in a 50:50 mix of perlite and peat.

All this publicity and interest in the in-between roses has meant that a whole new area of rose breeding has arrived. In the next few years we will see a range of these roses which will incorporate all that is good with the miniatures as well as the floribundas and hybrid teas. Some breeders are going further back into the old-fashioned garden and tea roses. Ralph Moore has already introduced the breeding of a very famous tea rose, Saffrano, into his line of miniatures. There is no limit to the types and colours that will be used in crosses.

In Ireland, Pat Dickson, already known for internationally famous hybrid tea varieties such as Red Devil and Grandpa Dickson (Irish Gold), is regarded as the man with the head start over other contenders such as Poulsen of Denmark and Ilsink of Holland, both of whom have already produced some winners in this range. What these breeders have in mind are small-growing bushes with masses of long-lasting blooms in all colours. Pat Dickson's seedlings are mainly in the apricot-orange-yellow blends and certainly carry through the idea that the bushes should produce masses of flowers right

through a nine month season. These bushes will be somewhere under 60cm (24in) in height with flowers that begin as miniatures but when fully open are almost as big as a normal-sized floribunda.

There can be no doubt that this range of roses will be a valuable addition to the small gardens and, of course, to patios. But what everyone seems to have forgotten is that there are a number of very good roses available already that fit exactly into this area and some have been around for quite a long time.

For instance, there is the old hybrid musk issued in 1937, Ballerina. Here is a super patio rose that has been confined to the garden up to now — and then only with enthusiasts for the old-type roses. The flower is small, single, light pink with a white eye, carried in huge clusters on a plant that you can keep low or allow to grow to 90cm (36in) high. I have grown Ballerina as a pot rose for a number of years and it sits beautifully on my patio, flowering its heart out without much assistance. It is a variety that you just cannot go wrong with and yet you will not see it advertised as being a good patio specimen. With me it is number one. For those who prefer a brighter colour, the deep red Marjorie Fair, bred from Ballerina, is remarkably similar in habit and equally promising.

Next on my list of favourites comes Nozomi, the climbing miniature, mentioned in earlier chapters, that comes from the Japanese breeder Onodera and was introduced in the late sixties. It has single, flat, pearly-pink flowers that grow in lovely trusses and it gets my award for the plant that is vigorous enough to bloom anywhere. If you are interested in breeding it sets seeds; and if you want to take cuttings they will root without any bother.

Cecile Brunner, the original sweetheart rose, is also a true winner. Regarded in some areas as a polyantha and in others as a hybrid China floribunda, it was issued as long ago as 1881. The bloom is small, fragrant, double, and bright pink when grown on a sunny ground. It can be bushy and dwarf or climbing or rambling and has a great habit of producing flowers forever, even though the foliage is often a little sparse. It is so effective that the great wonder is that it has been allowed to drift from many growers' catalogues. The very similar apricot-coloured shrub rose, Perle d'Or, is equally charming and free flowering.

Cecile Brunner has excited a lot of comment from dedicated rose followers who seem to be always in dispute about it and its relation to the climbing sport of the same name and another rose that looks very much like it, Bloomfield Abundance, which however makes a much taller bush. But don't let these little distinctions disturb you; the three versions are worthwhile growing. The only pity is that their sort doesn't seem to have been that easy to hybridise although some people do claim to have used Cecile both as a pollen and as a seed parent. If you ever try to breed your own rose you will soon find out that this is a very hard task to accomplish.

Quite different in style, growth and colour is Spong, named after the man who is said to have introduced it over a century and a half ago. Indeed, it seems to have been about before Mr Spong when it may have carried the stranger name of the 'Great Dwarf Rose'. Spong is a lovely little character rose, short, with pink, early-summer flowers, and is in the style of the pompon roses but comes under the group of centifolias, the old garden varieties known commonly as cabbage or Provence roses.

Nathalie Nypels small, decorative

and pink, is another in the old rose class. Introduced in 1919 it was originally named Mevrou Nathalie Nypels. It is noted for its continuous flowering and is quite attractive — when you get used to it.

Little White Pet, despite the fact that it is not classified as a miniature, often finds its way into shows under the miniature heading. It should, however, be with the old garden roses. Of all things it is a dwarf type of a rambler and carries clusters of pink-tinted buds which open to white and go on flowering right through to the end of the rose season.

While Cecile Brunner, Spong, Little White Pet and Nathalie Nypels typify the old garden dwarf growers, a far more recent arrival on the scene is the low-growing floribunda Regensberg, which certainly makes patio gardening a pleasure. Bred by Sam McGredy, it is a lovely combination of pink, white and silver. It is part of the line that he called 'hand-painted' roses because you seldom find two blooms with identical markings; they come in blotches, blobs, spots and stripes in a whole range of colours. Most of the others, some named appropriately for artists such as Picasso, grow too high for consideration in this chapter; but not Regensberg — it fits perfectly into my scheme of things. It flowers and flowers, the colours are exciting — and there is also a nice little story to tell about it. It was named for Lotte Gunthart, a famous flower artist who lives in the Swiss village of Regensberg, but before Lotte fell in love with the rose during a visit to the McGredy rose fields in New Zealand it was to be called Young Mistress. After all it is bred from Old Master, and Sam McGredy suggested that an old master deserved a young mistress.

Quite different from Regensberg are the 'Bell' roses bred by the Poulsen firm in Denmark. These carry small, loose floribunda flowers. There are Red, Pink and White Bells which each produce a mass of colour all season long and make ideal patio plants. Another European breeder, Peter Ilsink, is also well into the patio rose idea. His Robin Redbreast gives a good idea of what these roses should be like. The plant is low growing, the blooms are floribunda size and the colour is dark red with a white eye.

In England, Harkness Roses have produced quite a number of very effective roses which I have used as patio subjects. The shrub Yesterday is one of the best of these. Though the flower in this case is small the bush can be quite vigorous, but suitably cared for it can give huge trusses of beautiful fragrant lavender-mauve blooms. Another very pretty rose is the creamy-white Clarissa. Bolder in colour, deep orange with a touch of yellow, is Anna Ford, again with a semi-miniature bloom. This plant will grow well in a 25–30cm (10–12in) container. There is also Cocker's Wee Jock which produces the most perfectly formed scarlet flowers like small replicas of the famous hybrid tea Ena Harkness.

Angela Rippon also makes a good patio plant. While this rose can be regarded as a miniature, and is registered as such, it does tend towards a relationship with the in-betweeners and when bought as a budded plant certainly makes a height of 45cm (18in). It was bred by de Ruiters of Holland and introduced by Fryers in England.

Having mentioned these varieties it is worthwhile saying that just about any rose that doesn't grow too tall can be used as a patio subject. Where the modern roses are answering the call is with low growers that are bushy and prolific producers of flowers. There are a number of recently introduced floribundas that also fit this mould, notably Trumpeter (orange-red and a variety that goes on flowering all season long), Baby Bio (bright yellow), Warrior (bright red), Swany (white) and Bellarosa (pink). A significant pointer to the future is that both Anna Ford and Pat Dickson's canary-yellow, fragrant, bushy and low growing Ards Beauty (1983) won Royal National Rose Society Gold Medals as well as the supreme trials award The President's Trophy.

Further new varieties that certainly look as though they will add greatly to this class of in-betweeners are also worth a mention here. For instance, there is the range of de Ruiter rosamini and minimo roses which have the distinction in most cases of being perfectly formed and carrying great numbers of blooms all season long. Dwarf Fairy, Dwarf King and Dwarf Queen are varieties that are new from Kordes, but beware that they are not confused with the older roses of the same names that are still available in many catalogues — the new ones are taller but dainty enough to fit in most sections. Poulsen's Jennifer Joy, Golden Piccolo and Apricot Midinette are lovely specimens; Sam McGredy's Little Artist and Le Grice's Deb's Delight are others that should be considered.

Finally, a few words of warning. There is a very attractive low-growing variety called Tip Top that should be bypassed despite the pretty flowers. This variety has done more to put people off buying low growers than any other I know as it falls an easy prey to disease. And another group of low growers, the Compacta group introduced in the 1950s by de Ruiter, could also prove disappointing. Named for the seven dwarfs — Bashful, Doc, Dopey, Grumpy, Happy, Sleepy and Sneezy — they are disease resistant but lack good shape or colouring.

117

18

IN THE WORLD'S GARDENS

A mere decade ago there was hardly a rose garden in the world that would have given space to the miniature rose. Today, a public garden is nothing if it does not have even a small collection. At the Gardens of the Rose, in St Albans, Hertfordshire, there is an area especially for miniatures; in the beautiful gardens at Lyons in France, little roses provide interesting planting; in the Maori town of Rotorua, in New Zealand, there again you will find them; in Baden-Baden, in West Germany, special beds of miniatures are planted in the municipal gardens while the trial grounds have given an important place to them; and in America, where miniatures are becoming the fastest selling of all roses, most gardens are opening up to them.

Part of the fun of my travels throughout the world is to see as many rose gardens as possible. This is easy enough — the hardest part is making sure that I get to them when they are in full bloom.

The first garden I ever set out to see was the headquarters of the Royal National Rose Society in St Albans. Being a complete beginner in roses I set out the first week in June from my home in Dublin accompanied by my daughter, Siobhan. It was an expensive enough trip and I did want to get things right. Arriving in London, we took a bus and asked the driver to drop us off at a pub close to the gardens. He forgot, we were deposited miles north and had to hitch back. We succeeded but as we reached the gardens the heavens opened with a downpour heavy enough to drown a duck. Soaked to the skin, we scrambled into the gardens and received the final punch. There wasn't a rose in bloom! We were two weeks too early! So the lesson for the traveller was firmly imprinted on my mind that day: check with your travel agent before setting out, otherwise your trip may well be in vain.

The following short list of rose gardens throughout the world is necessarily selective — it would be virtually impossible to list them all. The dates given are for the main flush of bloom which is supplemented by a summer long display, and you can expect roses right through the autumn no matter where you go.

Great Britain

First flush of bloom: In the southern half of the country, June sets the seal on the roses; early July for the northern half; and in Scotland it is some time from the first week in July.

The Royal National Rose Society Gardens, St Albans, Hertfordshire Twelve acres of roses including a wide range of miniatures. Look especially in the trial grounds where the world's top hybridisers send their roses for testing.

New Rose Garden at Wisley, Surrey A place to see new varieties, which are being added to each year. As time goes by the miniatures will play an increasingly important part in the planting.

Springfields, Spalding, Lincolnshire A famous bulb garden that has joined ranks with the British Association of Rose Breeders. Improving all the time as new varieties are being planted.

Queen Mary Rose Garden, Regent's Park, London A magnificent rose garden but unfortunately not many miniatures as planting is for mass display on an eye-to-eye basis.

Provincial Display Gardens Many provincial parks now display new roses — these are situated in Cardiff, Edinburgh, Glasgow, Harrogate, Norwich, Nottingham, Redcar, Southport and Taunton.

Northern Ireland
First flush of bloom: July

Sir Thomas and Lady Dixon Park, Belfast This was the first rose garden to be established with the backing of Northern Ireland's rose firms, a very enthusiastic rose society and the Belfast City Council. Planted on gently sloping land, the garden, which is at its best in July, contains over 20,000 bushes many of them winners of the trials that are held here each year.

Irish Republic
First flush of bloom: Mid June

St Anne's, Dublin This garden on the north side of the city is the result of a great combination of work between the local rose society, Clontarf, rose growers in Britain, Europe and Ireland, and the Dublin Corporation. Beautifully kept, it hosts a rose week every year with prizes for the public in many competitions associated with the rose. This seems to me to be the ideally situated garden to create a miniature rose trial centre for the world.

North America
First flush of bloom: Depends on where you are. Roughly speaking the best times are May and September in most parts but the months in between will also have their share of roses. And of course the US has perfected the growing of miniatures to such an art that you will always be able to find them blooming somewhere.

United States
The American Rose Society produces a list of private and public gardens which welcome visitors in just about every state, ranging from 122 All America Rose Selection gardens right through to growers who have as few as fifty plants. For anyone travelling in the US, having such a list will make life so much easier. After all, who could pass through San Mateo without calling on Don and Mary Marshall (who each have a miniature named for them)? They have 300 roses and 300 miniatures in their garden on 28th Avenue and they welcome 'anyone, anytime'.

American Rose Center, Shreveport, Louisiana Opened in 1969, this garden is rapidly increasing its plantings of miniatures and probably has more of them growing in a garden and test ground than anywhere else that I know of. When completed, some 118 acres will be filled with roses.

Washington Park, Portland, Oregon A famous test garden with magnificent views. In 1978 a new miniature rose garden and test area was opened. The different varieties are grown in raised boxes for easy appraisal.

Park of Roses, Whetstone Park, Columbus, Ohio One of the national rose gardens, this park previously housed the headquarters of the American Rose Society. Over 13 acres of all sorts of roses.

Tyler Municipal Rose Gardens, Tyler, Texas Magnificent area of commercial rose growing. A very fine rose garden notable for a great Rose Festival. Miniatures certainly play their part here, being planted in raised beds.

Rose Hills Memorial Park Garden, Whittier, California A major centre for new roses, with miniatures in a dominant situation — it even has one named for it: Rose Hills Red. Two great rosarians were responsible for this garden, John von Barnaveld and James Kirk. By the way, don't be put off by the fact that the garden leads into a cemetery! Notable for a great annual Rose Show on Mother's Day. In 1984 it received a national best garden award.

Canada
Centennial Rose Garden, Burlington, Ontario Gardens that are both for pleasure and testing new varieties of the rose. If a rose is called to survive a hard winter this is where it can prove itself. One of the many new rose gardens that were the contribution of the 1960s to the beauty of the world.

Jackson Park Rose Test Gardens, Windsor, Ontario Again a garden from the 1960s with over 12,000 roses planted. The City of Windsor is so proud of its association that it has adopted the title City of Roses.

Dominion Arboretum and Botanic Gardens, Ottawa Extensive displays of roses of all sorts.

Butcharts Gardens, Victoria, BC, Connaught Park Rose Gardens, Montreal and the *Memorial Park Rose Gardens,*

Montreal make up the most important Canadian gardens. All the time interest in the rose is increasing and new gardens on a smaller scale are appearing in most cities and towns.

Europe
First flush of bloom: When you are in the south, around Spain and Portugal, the best times are from 15 May to 15 June. Going north from there the season varies from May right up to July when you will find the Danish roses at their best. France will be very good around the end of June. Germany, too, expects its roses to be at their best around about the end of June and the beginning of July.

Denmark
Valbyparken, Copenhagen Opened in 1963 it has about 20,000 roses in 300 different varieties.

France
France has long associations with the rose. Empress Josephine and the painter Redouté (1759–1840) created the great illustrated work *Les Roses* from the palace at Malmaison.

Today there are gardens everywhere but the main rose gardens are in Paris, Lyons, Bagatelle and Orleans.

La Roseraie de l'Hay-les-Roses, Paris Reckoned to be the oldest surviving rosery in the world, although it wasn't begun until 1893! Here they have tried to recreate some of Empress Josephine's collection and have provided a rose museum.

La Roseraie du Parc de Bagatelle Only two miles from the centre of Paris. Paved areas and carefully clipped box hedges make a lovely home for the rose.

La Roseraie d'Orleans Specialises in polyanthas, probably the forerunners of the miniatures where size is concerned. There is quite a collection of these on show here. Most of them are unobtainable commercially but they do provide an historical link with the rose growers of this area who made the polyantha their speciality.

La Roseraie du Parc de la Tête d'Or, Lyons This must rate among my favourites for the title of the most beautiful European garden. For those who become deeply involved with the rose, Lyons is a place of pilgrimage for it was here in 1858 that the great Joseph Pernet-Ducher was born. Eventually known as the 'Wizard of Lyons' he transformed the colour range of modern roses. His introductions include Soleil d'Or (1900) which brought yellow into the range of bedding roses. One of his famous roses, Mme Caroline Testout, is still on sale.

La Roseraie de Saverne, Strasbourg and *La Roseraie de Schiltigheim, Strasbourg* These two gardens are well worth visiting. The latter is a work of dedication by the local society Les Amis des Roses who maintain the grounds themselves.

Germany, East

The Sangerhausen Rosarium, Sangerhausen The most important rosarium in the world but unfortunately it is not easy to visit. The main theme of the rosarium is to preserve roses of value of all types and there are some 6,500 species planted here.

Germany, West

Insel Mainau, Bodensee (Lake Constance) Probably my favourite of all. The unique setting of a garden on an island provides a dream walk among roses of every sort. Sadly, the miniature hasn't really got a place here yet but there is no shortage of low-growing roses which can be seen in a garden setting. This is the type of rose garden where you need two days to go around — one to see the roses, the other to see the rosarians.

The City Rose Garden, Zweibrücken Another lovely garden where miniatures do get a good showing among the 60,000 roses planted. There is a fine tree-fringed park with a large ornamental lake.

The Rosarium of the German Rose Society, Dortmund Created in the last 15 years, this park is in the home of many modern roses.

Baden-Baden A city where you can see a number of rose gardens. The municipal gardens have a section devoted to miniatures where you can see such varieties as Baby Masquerade and Starina growing with vigour that can only surprise. And the trial grounds in the same city are well worth a visit — here you will see many of the new varieties and can make your own assessment of their performance.

Holland

Westbroekpark, The Hague Holland's main rose garden, featuring over 60,000 roses of all types including miniatures — a ready answer to those who think that Holland is only a country of spring flowers and bulbs. The display at The Hague lasts right through the summer months.

Italy

Italy boasts a great love of the rose as anyone who has ever visited their lake country in May and June will certainly testify.

Roseto di Roma, Rome The most important rose garden in the country. Originally planted in the ruins of Nero's Palace it was partially destroyed in World War II and a new site was taken on the Via de Valle Murcia on one of Rome's seven hills. About 1,000 different varieties can be seen here.

Villa Reale, Monza This is the site of another fine garden and trial ground.

Spain

El Rosaleda del Parque de Oeste, Madrid
Words can't really say how beautiful it is and it does give the miniature a very important place. This is not surprising as this is the land that gave birth to Pedro Dot, one of the fathers of the miniatures. They grow beautifully here in well-maintained surroundings.
Roseleda de Sevilla, Avda. Molini, Seville Some 7 acres are put aside as a very pretty park and here too the creations of Pedro Dot and Cipriano Compribi are featured.

Switzerland

Rose enthusiasts should consider a visit to Regensberg, near Zurich. It is a town of old houses, cobbled streets and flowers everywhere, but especially it is the home of Willi and Lotte Gunthart. Lotte is a famous painter of roses and was responsible for Sam McGredy naming his superb low-growing floribunda with its unusual combination of pink and silver blooms in honour of the town.
La Roseraie du Parc de la Grange, Geneva Set on the banks of Lake Geneva this is a credit to the country and is also many people's choice for the most beautiful rose garden in Europe. It is laid out on three levels, and you can get a marvellous view of the roses after dusk when the gardens are floodlit.

Australia

First flush of bloom: November and December.

I have yet to get this far down under but I am told that rose gardens are developing all the time. *The Victorian State Rose Garden*, east of Melbourne, is expected to be a real eye-catcher when it is completed. In the same area, but north of the city, is the *Benalla Rose Garden*, on both sides of a highway. *The Alistair Clark Memorial Rose Gar-*

den at St Kilda is also being developed. In Queensland there is the *New Farm Rose Garden, Brisbane*; in Tasmania both the *Hobart Botanical Gardens* and the *Rose Society of Tasmania Gardens* at Hobart are highly rated. In Adelaide, South Australia, the informal plantings at *Veale Rose Gardens* and, in New South Wales, the *Nellie Melba Memorial Rose Garden*, Sydney, are worth seeing.

New Zealand

First flush of bloom: November and December.

New Zealand National Rose Society Trial Grounds, Palmerston North Roses from all over the world take their chance in the trials held at this garden. The top award is greatly coveted. In 1983 the competition among the miniature entries was fierce — the winner being the Moore bred Sierra Sunrise.
Te Awamutu Rose Gardens, near Hamilton A small garden that is a blaze of colour all summer long.
Rogers Rose Garden, Hamilton A wonderful sight in natural surroundings, on the banks of the Waikato River.
Rotorua Rose Gardens Small but interesting for the number of miniatures. A town in the heartland where the tourist can see demonstrations of Maori culture.

South Africa

First flush of bloom: The first week in October.

South Africa has a number of interesting rose gardens but for miniature lovers the places to see all the newest varieties will be in Durbanville and Pretoria. In Durbanville the *Rose Garden* administered by the Western Cape Rose Society and personally supervised by Dick and Linda Lindner has some 2,500 plants of 100 different varieties growing. The *Pretoria Rosarium* has 1,500 miniatures planted. In both cases the severe droughts of recent times have held back the plantings and when conditions improve more miniatures will be included. Other notable rose gardens are the *Municipal Rose Gardens* in Cape Town and the *Johannesburg Botanic Gardens*.

Many of the gardens mentioned in this chapter have trial grounds attached. These are where the roses of the world are tested. The special miniature test garden at the American Rose Society's headquarters at Shreveport, Louisiana, is the only trial ground devoted entirely to the miniature.

However, most trial grounds have sections and special prizes for the best miniatures. Some, like the Royal National Rose Society, do not have category prizes and all roses are judged against each other. But as the surge towards the miniatures continues there will be, inevitably, more and more of them bidding for, and winning, the top awards.

19

THE BREEDERS — AND THE FUTURE

When anyone talks about miniature roses it will be a very short conversation before the name of Ralph Moore is mentioned. Other men such as de Vink, Dot and Thomas Robinson led the way before him, and no one would dare take the glory away from them, but it was this genial, shy Californian who took over the expedition and brought it triumphantly up to date.

As far back as 1936 Ralph Moore was breeding miniatures and despite the lack of interest shown by other breeders he stuck with it. For a long time he had the market virtually to himself. Kordes and Tantau in Germany, and Meillands in France joined him for a while but the Moore roses went on and on blazing their own path through the indifference of the rest of the rose trade.

For a little while in the 1960s the mighty Jackson and Perkins company in the United States took a few faltering steps but fell by the wayside and it wasn't until the early 1980s that it began to show a renewed interest in miniatures. By this time Ralph Moore was — and is still — the master hybridist. His gospel, however, was supported by the Dot family in Spain and picked up by many other growers; for instance, Saville in America, Gregory in England and Meillands in

France. Today there are dozens of commercial breeders of miniatures in the world but it is still to Ralph Moore that everyone looks for guidance and for a glimpse of the future.

During the past ten years or so I have met Ralph Moore annually somewhere in the world and we have talked miniatures. I am always amazed at his ability to recall immediately the roses that led to such a great line of breeding. A cross of an early seedling with the famous Tom Thumb produced the start of his line, a little rose called Zee. From this came Pink Cameo, Little Buckaroo, Westmont, Magic Wand and later Little Flirt, Yellow Doll, Mona Ruth and so many others.

Ralph cannot, however, put a finger on the time he started his love affair with the miniatures. He remembers roses all the way through his life; he remembers, too, the lack of interest most nurserymen showed in his little roses when he produced them. They were the 'ugly ducklings' of the rose world. But from 1960 onwards, miniatures and Ralph Moore began to make great inroads into the gardens of the world. He was helped a great deal in his international role through association with the late Walter Gregory in England who added the little roses to his formidable list long before they

were considered worthy of a place in garden or home.

Every year in the Sequoia Nurseries in Visalia they plant thousands and thousands of seeds. These are the results of what Ralph Moore calls his mental blueprint, a series of crosses extending over a number of years. But what is he looking for and what are his hopes for the future?

Like all the other people involved in miniature hybridising, he wants a rose that grows easily, is disease free and has elegance, pleasing form and a good colour. Novelty has to come high on the list too. Here the Moore introductions have been scoring with such unusual striped combinations as Stars 'n' Stripes, Strange Music and Earthquake. And there are more to come: orange and white, purple and silver; colours striped and mottled and blotched.

Ralph Moore began his series of striped roses sometime in the 1970s. He has carried this colour breakthrough to the moss roses as well. These heavily prickled little roses are a real throwback to roses that have been with us for centuries. Ralph produced Fairy Moss in 1970 and that was the

Perfection in bud – three tiny roses that caught my attention when visiting Ralph Moore's Nursery in California. The rose has not been introduced but is a lovely combination of purple and mauve stripes.

start of a line that achieved international acclaim with the lovely light pink, Dresden Doll. Since then he has gone through the pinks, reds, yellows and now even into the striped moss.

Another area where Ralph Moore achieved a great breakthrough was in the climbing miniatures with the likes of Pink Cameo, Little Girl and Red Cascade. Again, there is promise of more and better ones to come in this range.

While Ralph Moore gives credit to Dot and de Vink for the pioneering in the world of miniatures, Sam McGredy is just one of those modern breeders who turned to Moore for inspiration. McGredy, who has only come lately into the miniature breeding industry after a lifetime of producing world-beating hybrid teas, floribundas and climbers, will admit right away that without the help of New Penny, an early and very good Moore variety, he would never have bred

125

Anytime, a strange brick-red coloured variety that is the base of many of the McGredy miniatures. It is his opinion that: 'No one has done as much as Ralph Moore to improve miniatures and to make them popular. He was dreaming of miniatures when none of the rest of us bothered.'

McGredy realises that the little roses have a fantastic future and is always on the lookout for novelties. He too is well into the production of striped varieties and others with spots and speckles in just about every shade of the rainbow. Again he harks back to the Moore rose Stars 'n' Stripes as the instigator of his new ones but he is also able to include the whole complicated breeding that went into producing his 'hand-painted' floribundas Picasso, Old Master, Regensberg, Sue Lawley and the like. His first 'hand-painted' miniature to appear in Britain, code named Macmanly, in its second year in the RNRS trials was awarded a Trial Ground Certificate, a distinction hard to earn.

Ko's Yellow, Freegold and Wanaka are just three of the miniatures that pushed Sam McGredy further and further into the hybridising of them. He had so many when I visited him in New Zealand in November 1983 that he had a vase of a different variety in every room (even the smallest room). There are a great number of very good new miniatures to come from the experienced hand of this master as he marries the best that are available into his own very personal line of breeding.

While the McGredy idea of the future is of miniatures so adaptable that they will grow anywhere, the Meilland house in France is well set into the 1980s with varieties that they sell almost on the lines of house plants. In major stores throughout the UK the Sunblaze range of roses (Golden, Yellow, Pink and so on) have been big selling items since the start of this decade. The plants come in pots, usually four cuttings that have been grown in the one pot and so they have plenty of growth and blooms. Throughout Europe, Meillands, with Meillandina roses, as they call their own personalised range, do a great job of promoting the miniature.

You can buy the Meillandina range in different types: budded plants in 2-litre 16.5 x 15cm (6½ x 6in) pots, grafted plants in 10 x 12cm (4 x 5in) pots and rooted cuttings in 9cm (3½in) pots. This is worth noting because most nurseries today are merely offering the roses from cuttings, except in the UK where budded miniatures are still probably more often the rule.

But Meilland's history of producing miniatures goes back quite a long way and includes such little wonders as Starina and Darling Flame. Darling Flame has been used by many hybridisers, probably most successfully by Jack Harkness, the English breeder. The Harkness firm also marketed the lovely Peek-a-Boo (Brass Ring) from Pat Dickson in Northern Ireland. This was, I believe, the first miniature from the Irish master of the hybrid teas (Red Devil, Grandpa Dickson, Precious Platinum and others) and it quickly took off. But this is only a starter for Dickson whose new breed of in-between roses has been discussed earlier.

It is probably true to say that today there is hardly a rose grower who isn't selling some miniatures, either his own or those of another hybridiser. In Europe, famous breeders include Tantau (Baby Masquerade was probably his best mini and his bigger roses include such greats as Fragrant Cloud and Super Star), Kordes (Little Sunset, Bonny and many more promised), Spek (Sunmaid), Cocker (a number of new varieties in the pipeline), Mattocks (Gold Pin) and Fryers (hybridising on their own and also introducing other breeders' roses).

The Dutch family of de Ruiter has been associated with roses for many years and the challenge of the miniature has certainly been taken up by Gijs de Ruiter. His earlier successes include Crimson Gem, Blue Peter and Angela Rippon which is highly regarded the world over. In California recently it received a rating of 8.0, although few plants were available. In South Africa, Ludwig Taschner, secretary of the World Federation of Rose Societies, called it the country's 'absolute superior miniature'. Indeed, it grows so well there that even its breeder could not believe its fantastic performance when he visited the country in 1983. In Britain, too, it gets high rating. Certainly it would have to be one of my favourite bedding miniatures for the amount of bloom it produces.

In the de Ruiter scheme of things potted miniatures, as well as varieties that will produce small hothouse blooms, are the top priority. His Rosamini series — with prefixes such as Charming, Velvet, Red, Pink and other colours — is producing blooms which are said to be bringing higher prices in the world's markets than the normal large-sized hothouse blooms. Varieties in the Minimo range, also bearing colour prefixes, are expected to be the forerunners of the miniature as the 'perfect' house plant. One grower told me that in his opinion Gijs de Ruiter's varieties are as yet unsurpassable for growth, flowering ability and health, and there is not much more you can ask from any plant.

In the United States the firms of Jackson and Perkins, Armstrongs and Conard-Pyle are racing through with their own contributions to the miniature world.

Conard-Pyle can take a bow as being one of the first companies to take the miniature seriously in the United States by introducing de Vink's Tom Thumb and is now very much in business with both miniatures and the little 'in-between' roses. As Star Roses it introduces the Meilland roses to the American public as well as varieties from Benjamin Williams of Maryland who has been working for a long time on the in-between range. Potted up, Conard-Pyle roses such as Amber Flash, Stardance, and the Sunblaze range from France, are presented as perfect forcing roses. The company's slogan is: 'caring makes a world of difference.' Apply it to your miniatures and see the success it will bring.

Jackson and Perkins once had a hold on the miniatures in the 1960s when it introduced the lovely Little Betsy McCall bred by its then hybridist, Dr Dennison Morey, but for some reason let it slip. Now it is very much back in the hunt with its own varieties. Its hybridiser, William Warriner, who has won so many prizes with hybrid teas and floribundas, has produced Bojangle, Razzmatazz, Gumdrop and Funny Girl.

The J and P plants are slightly different from the output from other nurseries in that the rooted cuttings are grown on in field conditions for a year before being sold. Then the plants are sold in the same condition as normal bare-root roses — dormant but on their own roots. Not all rose growers agree that this method is best, but one wouldn't really expect them to; after all they are in opposition to one another. Their response to the J and P package was that any plant you bought would be just as big after one year in a pot as it would after one year in a field. A lot of people feel that the experiment may well be a breakthrough in the presentation of own-root miniatures and only time will tell whether J and P's operation really works.

There has been great rivalry over the years between J and P and Armstrongs. Both firms have their main operation centred in California and in the matter of miniatures certainly Armstrongs has been laying down the challenge with some very good varieties in recent years. With a forceful young man, Jack Christensen, as its hybridiser, Armstrongs have produced the very good Holy Toledo, a rich apricot, that won the hearts of miniature lovers immediately it came on the market. They also have Cricket, a bright orange, and the yellow Hopscotch. And they have been keeping up with the introduction of moss miniatures, presenting the public with Honey Moss, Heidi and the deep crimson Honest Abe. Like so many of the other breeders, the promise from these producers is also for a whole world of striped miniatures in the near future.

Harmon Saville, of Rowley, Massachusetts, is the best example I know of how roses can change your life. A one-time commercial fisherman who later went into mail order merchandising, he found that roses were taking up an increasing amount of his time. When the mail order business came to a halt the roses came out from the background and it wasn't long before Harmon had his own business, Nor' East Miniature Roses, set up. The initial orders were few and far between but then publicity started to come his way with mentions in such prestigious outlets as *Good Housekeeping* and the *New Yorker*. The business boomed, he introduced many of the best miniatures produced by amateurs and eventually had his own collection to put on the market.

The Saville operation took a giant expansion step in 1983 when over an acre of greenhouses were leased in California from the famous Armstrong Nurseries, and today the east and the west coast operations serve the whole country with an output of some 600,000 potted plants each year! And it's growing still. The influence of the Saville-bred miniatures is being noted in Europe where the Meilland house has put some of the Rowley roses on its lists with top publicity going to Mark One (Savamark), a brilliant, profuse orange that makes a marvellous mass-planting variety.

Also consistently successful with his miniature creations is Ernest Williams of Mini Roses in Dallas. Ernest, the quiet man of hybridising, also began his business as a hobby. His goals are brilliant colours, exciting bloom form with good substance and colour stability, disease resistance, heat and cold hardiness and plants that are able to renew themselves. He has produced varieties that certainly carry all these attributes, all stemming from his early realisation that Over the Rainbow was going to be a great parent — thus providing another link back to Ralph Moore who bred this rose. Since then the list of winners from Ernest Williams reads like a list of the top miniatures: Starglo, Hula Girl, Gloriglo, Red Beauty, Rose Window, Kathy Robinson, and one that he feels is his best yet, Loveglo.

Strangely enough, most of the work in hybridising has been a male preserve with the exceptions of Mme Meilland in France; Mrs Ann Cocker in Scotland, who has played a prominent part in the business since her husband's death; Betty Jolly in the United States who has been involved in the introduction of some very good new varieties; and in Southern California, Dee Bennett of the aptly named Tiny Petals Nursery, who has been hybridising for a number of years but has only recently been winning public acceptance of her varieties. Her big moment came in

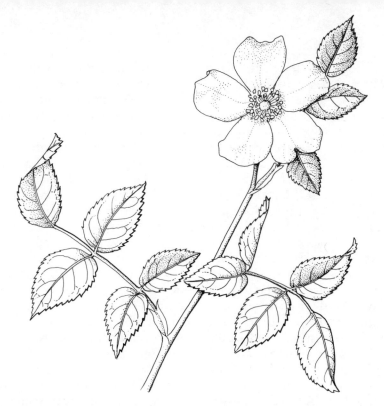

1984 when her lovely orange-red hybrid-tea-shaped mini, Hot Shot, won an Award of Excellence from the American Rose Society.

Dee Bennett's list of own-produced miniatures has a look of real substance about it now with such new varieties as Jean Kenneally, My Delight, Pops, Pucker Up, My Sunshine (a 1985 introduction), Starstruck (like the climber Joseph's Coat in that the flowers begin yellow and finish a deep red so that you have many colours on the bush at the same time) and Sugar 'n' Spice. Her older varieties have also made a great contribution to the acceptance of the miniature as a grow-anywhere plant — these include Ada Perry, Angel Dust, Cupie Doll, Georgette, Rosy Dawn and many others. Just how well the Dee Bennett roses have been taking their place, among miniatures in the US can be gauged by the fact that at three consecutive shows in California in 1984 her varieties won Queen of the Show title: Plum Duffy, Jean Kenneally and

Punkin. It only has five petals but, even in a tiny bloom, these manage to give a real rainbow range of colour. Orange with a yellow eye when first open, they go through deep orange to finish almost scarlet. One of the many new roses from Dee Bennett.

Pucker Up. The last two had been on the market only six months when they picked up the awards and Plum Duffy has been a favourite of mine for some time.

Canada has not been noted as a rose breeding country, probably because for years gardeners there have been able to take in the best from the rest of the world. Also, they haven't had Plant Breeders' Rights there, but in recent times Keith Laver of Mississauga, Ontario, has introduced a number of his own roses to commerce.

Laver's programme involves making about 8,000 crosses a year from which he has been selecting only miniatures for introduction. But like breeders everywhere he has also been getting a· number of in-between varieties

129

which will be marketed. His first introductions were Baby Face (profuse flowering pink), Blueblood (fairly largish velvet red), Ice Princess (pink fading to greenish white) and Ontario Celebration (a highly scented, vivid orange, chosen as Ontario's official bicentennial rose). And also like breeders everywhere, Keith Laver hopes that he may have the perfect indoor pot plant among his roses. He calls this group Potluck Roses. The potluck may well rub off on some of his other roses — Poulsens in Denmark and Saville in the US were the first to pick up the Laver-bred miniatures and market them. And the future? He believes the 'hand-painted' miniatures will provide an enjoyable variance from straight colours, and that the ground cover and cascading types of roses will be among the great innovations of the 1980s.

Many people expressed the belief in the 1970s that Japan and China would be the countries to produce a great new race of miniatures but apart from Japan's Onodera with Nozomi no significant varieties have so far come from these countries. In China, home of many of the original tiny roses, they know of only about twelve varieties. However, in the Hushan Rose Gardens in Cixi, Chekiang Province, a great deal of experimenting has been going on for a number of years and Mr Shi Chuan from there may be the man to introduce something new.

That takes care of most of the breeders. Some will, of course, have been omitted from this chapter, mainly because they have arrived lately on the scene and may still have to prove themselves in the field of miniatures. But what if you want to join their ranks? What should you be looking for in the future of these little roses?

Strangely enough, there doesn't seem to be anyone with a great vision of something really exotic or wonderful. Maybe outside the reality rose breeders do dream, but their thoughts and hopes are usually centred on logical things.

My own dream would be of a wonderfully fragrant blue miniature. And I would love to be the person to breed it — mainly, I must say, to enjoy the millions of pounds it will bring to its breeder; for that is what the first true blue rose will be worth. I have been breeding miniatures for years now and have come close: mauves and lavenders in the darkest tones, but never the blue. Will it come? That's a question that has been asked since man began to write about the rose. Most people say 'no' but there are a few dreamers who say 'yes . . . and maybe even tomorrow'. I believe that every rose breeder has a line upon which secret hopes are pinned; and from that line comes a number of little roses every year in the various tones just off blue, and from their seed sisters and brothers come pinks galore, reds, whites, yellows and creams. That is the way nature plays its own colour game. You could breed a line of four bluish roses together and get nothing but pinks. You could breed two pinks and get a lavender.

What about fragrance? Miniatures are not as yet blessed with full rose fragrance. The blooms are too small to carry a great deal but when the air is right and you put your nose into a bloom of Rise 'n' Shine I will swear you will have a fragrance. That is the next step among the breeders — to work on the fragrance of these little ones. Success will come probably a lot quicker with this than with the blue rose. Fragrance, though, can be just as exclusive in breeding as a colour. You can put together two of the world's most fragrant roses and get not a sniff from the seedlings. But use one of these non-fragrant seedlings back into a breeding line and it could well carry a most wonderful line of scent.

So you can see that there is plenty for the hybridisers to aim for. If you asked most of them, however, they would put both the blue rose and the fragrant miniature far down their list of plant priorities. They all say that what you want first of all is disease resistance. Breeders know how easy this is to lose and how, if roses become too in-bred, whatever resistance they have at the moment could be lost. So a rose breeding programme has disease resistance as a built-in necessity.

The world's breeders would also agree with the following goals: hardiness to both rain and sun; growth that is good to look at whether it is on the ground or in a hanging basket; repeat flowering (already most miniatures will give you three or even four crops of blooms during the season but continual flowering is vital); blooms that shed their petals quickly and don't set hips, because when hips are set the roses lose their flowering ability; roses that grow as well in a pot as any other plant; exciting new colours.

I have seen most colour combinations somewhere around the world in recent years — it is an exciting new phase for the miniature. For instance, if Jack Harkness can overcome the mulish qualities of *Rosa hulthemosa*, there will be roses with a red eye or centre.

And Sam McGredy has talked about a different type of rose, one that produces blooms like a delphinium with long spikes of really colourful flowers. Strangely enough, I had a number of these among my seedlings one year but I didn't see their value and discarded them. Another time I had (and still have) a lovely plant with salmon petals, red blotches in the petal centre, a yellow eye and silver reverse. But again I failed to believe that it had any potential and then Sam McGredy flooded the market with his 'hand-painted' varieties. So knowing what is marketable is very important. An eye for a potential winner is vital. In 1983, Ralph Moore produced a fairly straightforward-looking little semi-double, red with a yellow centre, the sort of bloom that few amateurs would look at twice if it was among their seedlings. He wondered if he should introduce it because it bloomed so well. Someone said: 'Why not?' So he did, calling it Why Not. It sold well in its first year though its true success has yet to be determined.

This is what makes the miniature so fascinating. When someone talks to me about the romance of the rose I know that it hasn't really reached its highest point. The best is still to come.

APPENDICES

1 DIARY FOR A MINIATURE-ROSE GROWER

When writing this book it was not always possible to avoid giving times of the year for certain chores and I am very conscious that in many parts of the world there will be great seasonal differences in the rose calendar. For instance, when I talk about taking cuttings in Britain I know that in Australia and New Zealand and in parts of the West Coast of the USA gardeners will be carrying out quite different tasks.

This brief summary of month-by-month work in the miniature-rose garden is written from a European point of view as far as dates are concerned. So when you are taking your cuttings 'down under' in January or February, in other parts of the world most plants will be completely dormant. Dates will be relevant in most parts of the US, where the only great difference is that after pruning most plants make a quicker run towards blooming than they do in Europe, and there is also a summer dormancy in many places that is unknown in Europe.

January
This is the time to look over all your plants, especially in places where there may have been high winds. If there has been any movement around the base of

the plant or if hard frosts have lifted the soil then make amends now. Press the soil firmly in around the roots; I often take some well-mixed soil in a barrow and fill in the places where movement is obvious. If you haven't done your planting earlier (I like to get plants in place by October–November to give them a chance to establish themselves before the spring push comes along) do it now whenever the weather conditions permit. If you do receive bare-root plants you can put them aside for a week or so if the roots are adequately covered with damp peat (or even damp newspaper). If the ground is frozen then you must hold off and the best way to look after your plants is to heel them in somewhere sheltered in the garden and cover them with soil. Remember to place a marker where you have put them — it is amazing how holes can appear in a gardener's memory!

February
'February fill-dyke' in most parts of the world can indeed be the wettest month of the year. But unless your soil is heavy clay you can continue to plant whenever the opportunity presents itself. This is also the month to look

over the plants and see what you can do to make the pruning task easier. If wood is broken, dead or hit by frost, cut it out of the plant now. If stems are too long, cut them back; but in most areas the final pruning is left for next month. Pots can be moved into greenhouses now but will need a temperature of 4°–7°C (40°–45°F). In a cold greenhouse full pruning can get under way.

March

Everything seems to be crying out for help in the garden! Pruning must be completed, all planting in open situations with bare-root roses should also be completed. Pots in the greenhouse will be growing well and the first signs of aphids will be present. Spray with a good insecticide; and give some liquid plant food in the watering can. You may need to make things a little warmer in the greenhouse to get the best from the plants. Among the plants growing outdoors the time is here to put on the first fertiliser but do make sure that you have cleaned the beds thoroughly first. Get out weeds, hoe the soil and then lightly spread a fertiliser around the newly pruned bushes.

April

Some northerly rose growers may have to wait until this month to get the pruning finished but in most other places it will be over and done with. If you still have to spread a fertiliser you must take more care now — don't let the powder or granules fall on any new growth as it will probably burn it. Gently hoe around the plant to incorporate the fertiliser. It is also time to consider spraying with one of the new multi-purpose sprays that will look after most needs of the rose and keep disease and insects at bay.

Pot roses will be starting into bloom

so continual care will be needed here. Keep them well watered, but not soaking, and watch out for spider mite. A good washing will help prevent a plague as will the use of an insecticide. The other main problem about now is mildew in the greenhouse, so your multi-purpose spray will be useful here too but don't spray in full sun.

May

The start of the great rose year. Some miniatures will begin to bloom now. In parts of the USA they will be right into the first flush and rose shows will have begun. If you are one of these lucky ones you should make sure that you have the schedule from your local secretary. If you are a first-timer you will get all the help you want. If you don't intend entering the show why not just go along and find out what it is like?

If you are going to mulch the beds (the best way to keep down weeds and to keep moisture in the soil) do it now. A lightweight material such as peat is good; cow manure (if old and well rotted) can be excellent but it is also generally so heavy that you can do damage to young growth putting it on now (see also page 47). Do not dig in the material, just leave it there to rot its own way into the soil.

The summer bugs are starting, so spray thoroughly. To get the best from your plants give them another feed of a fertiliser — a liquid fertiliser applied through a diluter will be very effective. If pot roses have finished blooming you can take cuttings (see Chapter 9). Dead-head them as you would other roses and you will have more blooms as the season goes on.

June

The month of the rose when you can enjoy finally the results of all those hours of work you have spent on them. Keep your eyes open for bugs and any signs of disease and do keep up a spraying programme. Don't spray in full sunlight, and try and pick a calm day to do this; if there is a wind about make sure that you wear a face mask — while I haven't heard of any of the normal sprays causing harm I haven't heard of them doing good either.

Rose shows are now getting into full swing everywhere. Do enter one — there is so much fun, and miniatures are simple to carry; remember never to let the blooms stand out of water for any length of time.

July

Continue to enjoy your miniatures but still keep a wary eye out for disease and insects. A monthly note that you should keep at the front of your mind is: don't let your roses dry out. They still need water and food as well as spraying. Don't be afraid to cut them when they are at their best. Generally speaking you can find more blooms going to waste in a miniature garden than anywhere else, yet half a dozen little flowers make a lovely tiny bouquet. And by cutting them you will be encouraging the next flush of blooms. Keep the weeds down.

From now on the cuttings you take should be just right to give you a whole barrage of new little plants. This is also the time to bud your own roses — miniatures are more fiddly than their big brothers but for the vigour of the eventual bush they are worth trying. If you want to hold back until next year you can look out for some stocks that you can pot up. Cuttings taken from a wild rose anywhere will root easily and you can have them ready for budding next year; some wild stock cuttings root so quickly that you could still plant them this month and bud them in September, although you should be warned that this is leaving the operation a little late.

August

My feeding plan means that the needs of the miniatures are looked after once a month, on the last day of each month, and this is the last month for feeding. It should be a light feed because you don't want to encourage too much new sappy growth that will be a victim of the first hard frost and could put your whole bush in danger. All through this month the same cultural techniques should be followed — spraying against disease and insects and hoeing down any weeds that still exist. This is a good month to take cuttings and root them for plants that will bloom next summer.

You can also start planning those new varieties that will grace your garden next year. Look around at growers' fields and look in on shows which will still be held in various places. Look, too, at other people's gardens and see what varieties of the mini they have growing — you might even be able to swap cuttings.

September

Still the miniatures are flowering and the more you cut for the house the more they will come again before the winter frosts arrive to send them into dormancy. Keep the weeds down, the insects away and don't think that now you can allow disease a free hand. The cleaner you keep your garden the better it is going to be next year. Don't be afraid to take cuttings still; they will grow and give very good plants.

Send off your order if you want new bushes; first in means first served and with the great interest in miniatures many growers find the best varieties disappear very quickly. If you are going to plant out new roses, start preparing the beds.

October

I look upon this month as potting-up

month. I go through all my plants and those that I want for early flowers are potted up and placed in a sheltered part of the garden away from too much late sunshine (but in enough to keep them moving). The pots will be left out until December when they are brought into the greenhouse or conservatory and encouraged to move along. Don't let them dry out.

My anticipation reaches its highest in October. I see now the places where a plant can be changed (but the soil must be changed too because a new rose should never be planted where one has been growing). I like to get an early planting too of any new varieties ordered and thus give them a good chance to settle into their way of growing before winter grips them.

Indeed, I find that there is more work to do in the garden now than in any other month. Cleaning, tidying, dead-heading and hoeing. This is really your last chance to take suitable cuttings. All little cuttings that have rooted should be moved into pots. To get the best results place about three rooted cuttings around a 12cm (5in) pot. Don't feed but make sure there is no carry over of summer insects looking for a winter home.

November

There will still be flowers to cut on miniatures in many places. I always expect to have some blooms for Christmas from bushes growing outside — and they will have been in bloom since May or June. Miniatures are generally more winter hardy than many roses but in very cold areas consideration will have to be given to covering them with some sort of protection if heavy frosts and snows are expected.

November is a good month to plant in most places. But if the weather isn't right when your roses are delivered then wait a while, heeling in the bushes until things improve. Make sure that all roses are firmly planted and kept damp, even in November they can dry out from cold winds. Now is the time too to put down a mulch of the heavier types of manure. You can work among the bushes more easily than you can in the spring and the mulch will keep the soil warmer and moister than it would be without it.

December

With luck you will have a Christmas bouquet of blooms. Don't be afraid to cut them and bring them indoors; they will last longer than most summer cut blooms.

Move your potted roses into the greenhouse or conservatory, where temperatures should be at least above freezing point. You can prune these now, taking away all the poor wood and making sure that the pots are not rootbound. Repot, clean and set the newly pruned bushes into their indoor environment for early blooms. After this you must tend them as you would the garden miniatures by spraying, feeding and watering.

Bushes in the open will be having a winter rest . . . and maybe it is time too for the miniature lover to sit down with a good book and plan what is ahead for the next year.

If you really want to know about roses you should join a local rose society. Every country seems to have its area and district societies and quite a few countries have national societies. These national societies produce regular bulletins and annuals, arrange shows and meetings, and many also promote rose trials where new seedlings are evaluated. The value from their publications alone makes these societies really worth the subscription; for instance, at the time of writing the American Rose Society annual subscription is $18 and the Royal National Rose Society's is £10.

Through your national society you will be able to find out the address of your nearest area society; or if you have a problem most national societies will have a local member with whom they can put you in touch.

At the top of the scale is the World Federation of Rose Societies which was founded in 1971 and elected as its first president Mr Frank Bowen, a former president of the Royal National Rose Society. The Federation holds meetings every two or three years — Baden-Baden in Germany was the locale for the 1983 meeting and Toronto for 1985.

The secretary/treasurer of the World Federation of Rose Societies is Ludwig Taschner, PO Box 28165, Sunnyside, Pretoria 0132, Republic of South Africa.

The national societies are as follows:

Argentina
The Rose Society of Argentina,
Solis 1255 (1686) Hurlingham,
Buenos Aires

Australia
The National Rose Society of Australia,
271 Belmore Road,
North Balwyn,
Victoria 3104

Belgium
Société Royale Nationale,
Les Amis de la Rose,
Mullemstraat 14,
B – 9762,
Mullem (Oudenaarde)

Bermuda
The Bermuda Rose Society,
PO Box 162,
Paget

Canada
The Canadian Rose Society,
20 Portico Drive,
Scarboro,
Ontario MIG 3R3

France
Société Française des Roses,
Parc de la Tête d'Or,
69459 Lyons, Cedex 3

Great Britain
The Royal National Rose Society,
Chiswell Green Lane,
St Albans,
Hertfordshire AL2 3NR

Holland
The Netherlands Rose Society,
Kievitweg 5,
5752PT Deurne

India
The Indian Rose Federation,
438, Pushpam,
10th Road,
Chembur,
Bombay 400 071

Israel
The Rose Society of Israel,
Ganot–Hadar,
PO Natania 42930

Italy
Associazione Italiana della Rosa,
Villa Reale,
20052 Monza

Japan
The Japan Rose Society,
4–12–6 Todoroki,
Setagaya-ku,
Tokyo 158

Luxembourg
Letzeburger Rousefrënn,
51 Ave du 10 Septembre,
Grand Duche de Luxembourg

New Zealand
The National Rose Society of
  New Zealand,
PO Box 66,
Bunnythorpe,
Palmerston North

Northern Ireland
The Rose Society of Northern Ireland,
'Gwynharoed',
13 Glen Ebor Park,
Belfast BT4 2JJ

Poland
The Polish Society of Rose Fanciers,
Warszawa 86,
Browiewskigo 19 M7

South Africa
The Federation of Rose Societies of
  South Africa,
PO Box 28188,
0132 Sunnyside,
Pretoria

Switzerland
The Swiss Rose Society,
Haus Engelfried,
CH 8158 Regensberg/ZH

United States of America
The American Rose Society,
PO Box 30,000,
Shreveport,
Louisiana 71130

West Germany
The German Rose Society,
Waldseestrasse 14,
7570 Baden-Baden

Zimbabwe
The Zimbabwe Rose Society,
33 Epping Road,
Mount Pleasant,
Harare

3 WHERE TO FIND THEM

There are very few countries left in the world where miniatures are not easily obtainable — nurserymen don't miss winners and most rose nurseries now carry a full complement of the little roses in their catalogues. Those who don't do this at the moment will certainly have to change their stock in the very near future when the great interest in the little plants rolls up to their doorsteps. As well as the general rose nurseries, specialist miniature growers have now arrived in big numbers, especially in the United States.

Of course, you will not find every variety that is mentioned in this book at more than a very few nurseries. The majority carry a special list of anything between thirty and a hundred varieties. Not many could provide you with the

500 varieties that appear in one Californian grower's catalogue.

If you want a variety that is impossible to obtain locally then you should turn to your local rose society. If you have no luck there then try the national society. Certainly the Royal National Rose Society in St Albans carries a computerised list of varieties and can provide you with a lead to the plant you want. So too can the American, Australian and New Zealand societies, and I am sure most other national societies will do the same.

If you want something that you can turn to at any moment there are a couple of useful publications.

First, there is *Find that Rose*, a very useful book issued by the British Rose Growers' Association. The booklet is inexpensive and at the time of writing the address is Rose Growers' Association, 303 Mile End Road, Colchester, Essex CO4 5EA. The booklet has its limitations in that it only lists members of the association and that does not include all rose growers in the UK.

A comprehensive list on an international scale is produced by Beverly R. Dobson, 215 Harriman Road, Irvington, New York, 10533. This has fifty pages listing roses in commerce and cultivation but its greatest asset is in providing names of outlets for hard-to-find varieties. Mrs Dobson did a magnificent job with the booklet which is the best source of such information that I have seen.

If you read these booklets you will probably be fired by enthusiasm and want to bring overseas material into your own country. However tempted you may be don't go doing it until you have looked up the national importation regulations. These are usually so red-taped that unless you are really dedicated to making the purchase you will probably decide that what you have in your own country is good enough.

4 THE BIG 'E' AWARD

The American Rose Society Award of Excellence is the top award for a miniature in the US. Test gardens have been established throughout the country at sites in Shreveport, Louisiana; Rose Hills, Whittier, California; Crosby Gardens, Toledo, Ohio; International Rose Trial Gardens, Portland, Oregon; and Denver Botanical Gardens, Denver, Colorado. Here the varieties are judged each month during the growing season for garden effect, colour, form, plant habit, health and general value in bloom production. To merit the award of a big 'E', the symbol chosen by the ARS, the variety has to be very good indeed.

Winners of the Award of Excellence up to 1984 are:

Beauty Secret (R. Moore) 1975
Judy Fischer (R. Moore) 1975
Toy Clown (R. Moore) 1975
Lavender Lace (R. Moore) 1975
Over the Rainbow (R. Moore) 1975
Sheri Anne (R. Moore) 1975
Magic Carrousel (R. Moore) 1975
Mary Marshall (R. Moore) 1975
White Angel (R. Moore) 1975
Starglo (E. Williams) 1975
Red Cascade (R. Moore) 1976
Hula Girl (E. Williams) 1976
Peachy White (R. Moore) 1976
Peaches 'n' Cream (E. Woolcock) 1977
Jeanne Lajoie (E. Sima) 1977
Gloriglo (E. Williams) 1978
Humdinger (E. Schwartz) 1978
Rise 'n' Shine (R. Moore) 1978
Avandel (R. Moore) 1978

Cuddles (E. Schwartz) 1979
Puppy Love (E. Schwartz) 1979
Red Flush (E. Schwartz) 1979
Zinger (E. Schwartz) 1979
Pink Petticoat (L. Strawn) 1980
Holy Toledo (J. Christensen) 1980
Party Girl (H. Saville) 1981
Pacesetter (E. Schwartz) 1981
Center Gold (H. Saville — best rose of 1982 but an 'E' award not possible because it had been selected as a special presentation variety for the American Rose Foundation)
Cornsilk (H. Saville) 1983

Cupcake (M. C. Spies) 1983
Hombre (N. F. Jolly) 1983
Snow Bride (B. Jolly) 1983
Valerie Jeanne (H. Saville) 1983
Baby Eclipse (R. Moore) 1984
Hot Shot (D. Bennett) 1984
Julie Ann (H. Saville) 1984
Little Jackie (H. Saville) 1984
Black Jade (F. Benerdella) 1985
Winsome (H. Saville) 1985
Jennifer (F. Benerdella) 1985
Centerpiece (H. Saville) 1985
Loving Touch (N. F. Jolly) 1985

5 WHERE TO BUY THEM

As the popularity of miniature roses has increased dramatically in recent years it has become almost mandatory for rose nurseries everywhere to include at least a small number in their catalogues. But there are also nurseries throughout the world that specialise in miniatures.

European hybridisers of miniatures such as Poulsen, Kordes, Meillands, Tantau, Spek and Ilsink have their own roses available through their own catalogues. They also have agents in other countries. McGredy and Dickson introductions are handled through agents in different countries, but can be found in many other catalogues as well.

This list merely touches the tip of the list of various nurseries which sell miniatures but it will, I hope, help to guide you to growers whom I can personally recommend.

UK
Anderson's Rose Nurseries, Friarsfield Road, Cults, Aberdeen

David Austin Roses, Bowling Green Lane, Albrighton, Wolverhampton WV7 3HB
Cants of Colchester Ltd, The Old Rose Gardens, London Road, Stanway, Colchester, Essex CO3 5UP
James Cocker & Sons, Rose Specialist, Whitemyres, Lang Stracht, Aberdeen
Fryer's Nurseries Ltd, Manchester Road, Knutsford, Cheshire WA16 0SX
Gandy's (Roses) Ltd, North Kilworth, Nr Lutterworth, Leics LE17 6HZ
Gregory's Roses, The Rose Gardens, Stapleford, Nottingham
R. Harkness & Co Ltd, The Rose Gardens, Hitchin, Herts
Arthur Higgs Roses, Water Lane Farm, North Hykeham, Lincs
LeGrice Roses, Norwich Road, North Walsham, Norfolk NR28 0DR
John Mattock Ltd, The Rose Nurseries, Nuneham Courtenay, Oxford OX9 9PY
Rearsby Roses, Melton Road, Rearsby, Leics LE7 8YP
R. V. Roger Ltd, The Nurseries, Pickering, North Yorkshire

Rosemary Roses, The Nurseries, Stapleford Lane, Toton, Beeston, Nottingham NG9 5FD

Star Roses (Meillands), 464 Goff's Lane, Goff's Oak, Waltham Cross, Herts EN7 5EN

Timmermans Roses, Lowdham Lane, Woodborough, Nottingham NG14 6DN

Warley Rose Gardens Ltd, Warley Street, Great Warley, Brentwood, Essex

Wisbech Plant Co Ltd, Walton Road, Wisbech, Cambs

USA

Armstrong Nurseries, PO Box 4060, Ontario, California 91761.

Gloria Dei Nursery, 36 East Road, High Falls, New York 12440.

Justice Miniature Roses, 5947 SW Kahle Road, Wilsonville, Oregon 97070.

Jackson and Perkins, Medford, Oregon 97501.

McDaniels Miniature Roses, 7523 Zemco St, Lemon Grove, California 92045

The Mini Farm, Route 1 Box 501, Bon Aqua, Tennessee 37025

Miniature Plant Kingdom, 4125 Harrison Grade Road, Sebastopol, California 95472.

Mini Roses, (Ernest Williams) Box 4255A, Dallas, Texas 75208

Mini Rose Nursery, PO Box 203-D, Cross Hill, SC 29332

Moore Miniature Roses, 2519 E Noble Ave, Visalia, California 93277

Nor'East Miniature Roses, (Harmon Saville) 58 Hammond St, Rowley, Mass. 01969

Rosehill Farm (N. Jolly), Great Neck Road, Box 406A, Galena, MD 21635.

Star Roses, Conard Pyle Co, West Grove, Pennsylvania 19390

Tiny Jewels, 9509 N Bartlett Road, Oklahoma City, OK 73111.

Tiny Petals Nursery (Dee Bennett), 489 Minot Ave, Chula Vista, California 92010.

Canada

Springwood Miniature Roses, PO Box 255, Port Credit, PO Miss, Ontario L5G 4LB

Australia

Roy H. Rumsey, 1335 Old Northern Road, Dural, NSW 2158

New Zealand

Southern Cross Nurseries, PO Box 12009, Christchurch.

South Africa

Ludwigs Roses, PO Box 28165, Sunnyside 0132.

INDEX

142